*True Stories and Tough Lessons about a Small Business
that You Won't Learn in a Classroom*

Advance Praise

"In sharing her own story, Sarah Y. Tse provides insightful guidance about some of the pitfalls business owners need to be aware of. She shares honestly and isn't afraid to identify the mistakes she has made."

"*7 Years on the Front Line*™ is a 'shotgun' of summary stories with advice unlike a long-winded textbook of models, graphs, interpretations with esoteric words.'"

"Being a slow (& impatient) reader, the short but intense stories kept me going - hard to put it down.... all the stories are attractive lessons."

"Awe in how, after 7 years, everything played out to God's glory and Sarah's good; relief because there were justice and peace at the end of these trials; and conviction toward the areas I need to be cautious of in my life."

"Sarah's stories really empower and teach the readers without trial and error on how to be a wise business leader/owner."

"This book is creative in that it reaches out to people not only in business but also those who are intimidated by the legal system of this country."

*True Stories and Tough Lessons about a Small Business
that You Won't Learn in a Classroom*

FR◉NT
7 Years on the
LINE

Sarah Y. Tse

TSE Worldwide Press, Inc.

Rancho Cucamonga, CA

ISBN: 978-0-578-49421-0 (Hardback)
Library of Congress Control Number: 2019908398
Printed in China
First printing edition 2020

Cover design: United Yearbook® Printing Services, Inc.

Author: Sarah Y. Tse
Collaborator: Dr. John K. Tuttle
Editor-in-chief: Donna Ladner

This book is dedicated to my mother

and

in loving memory of my earthly father.

CONTENTS

1

INTRODUCTION

"You are a worm! Go back to China!" His words exploded out of the speakerphone and echoed off the conference room walls. Hearing the commotion, my employees in the surrounding offices poked their heads out of their office doors and looked at me in shock. The man on the phone kept yelling at me: "You are a Chinese worm!"

I had been running my own publishing company for 18 years and had developed a reputation in the industry for designing and delivering unusually formatted books: children's books in the shape of animals, die-cut books with buckles and straps, and books with special finishes and embossing. Designing unique book packaging was my passion and specialty. I helped my clients turn their conceptual ideas into reality. One of my books, a collaboration with my brother, a mechanical engineer, came in a large egg carton and was profiled by the managing editor of the New York Times Magazine in a two-page spread. The exposure and publicity allowed the book's author to sign a deal with a major publisher in New York and a multimillion-dollar licensing agreement with a high-end kitchenware company.

The man currently on the phone was part of a new project I was working on; a major airline wanted to produce a book they could give to children boarding their flights. They had contracted with a well-known art director at a reputable New York ad agency to design a book shaped like a child-sized briefcase. The art director then contacted me: he would create the initial layout and my company would print the book. However, when it came time to print, there were serious discrepancies between the specifications he sent and what he said he wanted to achieve, so I recommended some changes.

He was not happy to hear me point out his errors. It was at this point when he started shouting through the speakerphone: "You are a worm! Go back to China!" After the third or fourth time of this outburst, I had had enough. I interrupted him and said, "I am sorry, but speaking to me like that is not acceptable. I will disconnect you."

He continued, "You are a worm! Go back to China!"

I replied, "Look, I don't want to be rude, but my employees are here and can hear you screaming. I will hang up if you do not stop."

He did not stop, and I followed through. I hung up on him. Talking about the incident, first with my staff and later with my friends on social media, I felt more shock than anger. It shocked me to hear this language from a professional in a business setting and in the 21st century. I was disappointed that he received my good faith efforts in this manner. Over time, however, the story became a point of humor for myself, my staff, and my friends. I mean, worms do not have a nationality. You cannot look at a worm and tell if it is from Kenya, China, or America. The idea is absurd!

I share this story for two reasons, which together form the backbone of this book.

First, the phone call was not the worst thing that happened to me during a seven-year period that included business setbacks, personal losses, financial crises, and spiritual battles. There were endless litigations, and times when I nearly lost my company, and at one point I considered taking my own life. The art director's remark may have been the most dramatic moment of that time, but it showed me how I was often treated by others: as an outsider, an outcast, someone who didn't belong and who didn't deserve success. I felt like the biblical character David, only I faced more than one Goliath.

The second, and more importantly, these storms caused a process of change. I did not let these seven years make me a bitter person. Instead, I fought to come out a better person. My friends told me, "You are handling this so well and you have such a good attitude" and my staff told me, "This company is stronger because of all the chaos." This book is about the process of how that good attitude developed and I became a better and stronger person.

For years, my colleagues, friends, and family told me to write this book and tell my story.

Those words that afternoon summed up the voices I heard during my time in the wilderness: "You can't. You won't. You never will. Give up now."

But here I am, still standing, and here is this book.

If you are hoping to read a book about someone who overcame adversity by crushing her enemies, who won by learning to retaliate and fight harder, nastier, and dirtier than the big boys, then this book will be a disappointment; that is not my story.

It is not about how I became a "winner" by making someone else a "loser." As I write this, this nation and many other parts of the world are becoming more polarized, more divided, and so very concerned with winners and losers. Fights, conflict, and arguments make good TV. But that is not what this book is about. It is about perseverance, positivity, and courage. It is my attempt to encourage you to come through your own trials stronger. My desire is for you, the reader, to walk through new doors and reach for new opportunities, prepared for what is to come.

Throughout this book are nuggets of wisdom I have gained through my career running a small but growing business. It is my hope that they will be blessings to you. They are truths that evolved out of my faith journey and are an integral part of my life story. My understanding of God's love and purpose for me laid the foundation of my life. My value system and ethical perspective arose out of faith in a loving, personal God. I am excited to share the powerful insights that came out of my transformative, difficult life experiences. It is my hope that they will bless and guide you in your unique life journey. There are opportunities to apply this wisdom every day—including in my encounter with the art director.

What happened to him? He tried to call, email, and reach me via LinkedIn. He left several messages, never apologizing, always acting like nothing had ever happened, and asking me to continue the project. I made the choice to never respond, and I never charged him a penny, even though I had constructed a full prototype. I just didn't need the drama.

And that book he wanted? Ironically, it was a book for kids about airplane etiquette and how to behave politely on a flight.

2

GUT FEELINGS

August 19, 2011 was a significant day; it marked a turning point in my life. It was the first day of a cycle of trials that lasted for almost seven years.

The day began in Hong Kong, where I received the key to our brand-new office building. Excited about my future, I answered what I thought was a casual phone call from one of my biggest clients. It sent everything into a tailspin. Dana, the Co-CEO, informed me something was wrong with the product I had just delivered. This was definitely not what I expected or wanted to hear.

This relationship began in 2006, when Danielle, Dana's sister, and her mother, Nancy, created an innovative product, which despite its amazing potential, suffered from poor execution. The company was a start-up with limited financial resources; they had been working with another manufacturing and packaging company when one of my employees directed them to us. It was a family business primarily run by Dana, Danielle and Nancy. They lived on the East Coast and my company was in Southern California, which meant that our initial business was all over the phone. Based on these telephone conversations, I, along with my mother, brother and youngest sister, developed a prototype to help redesign and re-engineer their product and packaging. Although the project was complicated, we were satisfied with the results.

A few months later, in early 2007, I finally had the opportunity to meet Danielle. She flew to California, and we met at my office. She was excited about the prototype and wanted to place a large order with us, one worth close to $3 million. This would be their very first order, and my staff and I were excited about working alongside them to make their dream come true. There was one complication: they were unable to pay the entire $3 million, or even an adequate deposit. They hoped I would be willing to contribute to the financing. I could not raise the entire $3 million, but I was comfortable advancing them $1.3 million.

We sealed the deal with a handshake: regrettably, I did not insist on legal paperwork to protect myself. It seemed like a good business decision at that time. I truly believed in their product and that it would take off quickly. I thought my investment would be covered and that we would have a long-term, mutually beneficial relationship. While their lack of funds caused some alarm bells to go off in my head, I chose to go ahead with the investment. I took a huge risk: my company was small and $1.3 million was a considerable amount.

Looking back, I realize I agreed by reason of my trust in Danielle, who told me she was a Christian, and her mother, Nancy, who co-created the product. From the start, both women communicated their faith and involvement in the church. Danielle and I even shared our service as youth counselors at our respective churches. Trust and friendship between our two companies was evident from the very beginning. Then, everything changed.

3

GOOD OR BAD?

A few months prior to the phone call from Dana which set everything in motion, I received the first clue that my relationship with the client had begun to change, and not for the better.

In February 2011, I welcomed Danielle, whom I had met back in 2007, her CFO, and new COO to my California office. The COO had been with a large national retailer for over 20 years and was an experienced administrator. The meeting concerned me a little; Danielle seemed dissatisfied with the quality of the items I had produced. This was the first time in over four years she had mentioned any issues, and, oddly, she didn't give any specifics about what seemed to be wrong, just that she wasn't happy. Soon, however, it became apparent that the executive team had an ulterior motive: they wanted to ask for more financing, quite a lot more. Their company had grown to the point of opening overseas branches and having products in many stores, but they were again lacking in cash. At least, this was the story they told me. They requested close to $2.6 million.

There was another person who wasn't at that meeting but who had a major impact on its results. Danielle's sister, Dana, was now involved in the business. She had worked for a large television home shopping company and had extensive experience in marketing, branding, and licensing. Sales of their family's product exploded after she took over the marketing, but she conducted business much differently than her sister. She nitpicked and haggled over every cent spent, while prior to her participation we had the freedom to make choices in our client's best interests. She often asked things like, "Why are you spending $50 on this?" or "Why are you charging us $100 for that?" This sister was the one who hired the new COO in hopes of increasing marketing, both of the product I was working on and of the company overall. In that meeting, the COO was supposed to serve as a negotiator: to negotiate a larger financing deal and a no-interest loan from me.

This may sound strange, but even before the COO said anything at the meeting, I felt a great sense of evil in him. Notably, several of my employees immediately disliked him too. "This guy. . .there's something about this guy," one of them told me. With him, it was only about money. Up to this point, I had trusted the family and believed they had integrity, because they had opened up to me about their faith, goals, and struggles. I thought that trust was reciprocal, and that our working relationship was formed out of our common faith.

In August, I received a message from Dana that the initial shipment of products I had delivered was defective. Soon what had been a positive business relationship turned into an ongoing dispute. I called her back from my company's office in Hong Kong to determine the problem, and she proceeded to give a long list of what she felt was defective. I shouldn't have been surprised. In the six months between my meeting with the new executive team to this phone call, there had been several unusual emails.

First, I received an email from Danielle saying that she was visiting Hong Kong on vacation. I thought this was a little odd: she had a family—a husband, daughter, and son—and she was going on vacation by herself to Hong Kong? I should have suspected that it was not a vacation but instead a scouting mission.

Sometime later there was a corporate email from the COO, apparently accidentally cc'd to me, and giving key employees an update on their business in China. At the time, I thought the only business dealings they had in China was with me and my company. One of the addressees jumped out at me: my now former employee, the same one who introduced me to this client.

I didn't put together the pieces until later, but by the time I received the call informing me of my "defective" product, my former employee had already given them proprietary information she had taken before she left, including my design, construction specifications, trade information, and manufacturing sources.

The August phone call was still relatively friendly; but a week later, their "negotiator" COO got involved in the dispute. He informed me that the company would stop paying me, and they were keeping all of the product that had already been delivered. In October, I flew to their warehouse on the East Coast. They only allowed me to see a portion of the inspection line and very little of the product: they did not even allow me inside the warehouse. However, they continued to claim that several "certified lab tests" proved my product was defective. We scheduled a negotiating meeting for December in the hopes of reaching a settlement.

In December, I flew back to the East Coast and met with a local lawyer I hired to represent me. Oddly, an hour prior to the meeting with my lawyer, all my electronic devices—both my phone and computer—stopped working. It was a strange coincidence and a bad sign. And, when I walked into the meeting with my client's representatives, I felt an evil presence. After these signs I shouldn't have been surprised when I heard the settlement offer. The client wanted me to ship the remainder of their order from the Chinese manufacturer to their U.S. warehouse where it would be inspected. They would decide which items were worthy of payment based on this inspection and using criteria never explained to me. If they considered an item of adequate quality, I would be paid $0.50. They would then sell the same item for $29.95. This was added to the fact that I had already paid the manufacturer up front because the client didn't have the cash.

My immediate response was: "No, that's not going to work." I calculated that the company owed me $1.35 million, yet they had the nerve to offer me only $300,000. In addition, this deal allowed them to keep all the merchandise, "defective" or otherwise. At this point, a light bulb went on in my head: I realized they were never interested in negotiating a settlement. I was being played. I found myself pleading: "What is going on? I helped you to start this business while you were operating out of the lunch room at your father's office. I helped you design the packaging you are still using! What is going on? Why would you do this to me?"

4

TO THE BOTTOM AND BACK

The timing of the December meeting couldn't have been worse for me emotionally, financially, or spiritually. Prior to the meeting, I had already begun to feel a deep sense of betrayal. I had thought I could trust these people and that a handshake agreement would be enough. But now, after four years of a good relationship, I was being personally betrayed and financially ruined. I believed that all of my goodwill and positive intentions toward this company were being repaid with evil. Paralyzed with doubt, fear, and despair, I began to spiral downward. I thought: *This is all my fault. My product is awful, my company is a failure, everything is bad, and I'm the one responsible. I must have done something wrong, something horrible, to be treated so unjustly and unfairly.* My depression became such that I didn't want to get up in the morning. I couldn't face any more awful news. For the first time in my life, I contemplated suicide.

It was in this state of mind that I met with the client's executive team. During our meeting, the CFO pushed the settlement paperwork toward me in such a forceful manner that the papers fell off the table onto the floor. This provocation brought out my anger for the first time, and I said, "What do you think I am? You guys have your lawyer over there.

You have six people here. I came here by myself from California to try to resolve this. You throw this paper on the floor, and I'm supposed to pick it up like a dog?" I believed the team was treating me with the utmost disrespect. I even told my lawyer, "Do you see how they're treating me, and you're not going to say anything?"

My frustration knew no bounds. At this point, I told their executive team, "I'm done. We are done. I'm not signing anything, and I am leaving." I had wasted $25,000 on lawyer fees and airfare, plus my own time. The only result was the realization that my intuition was justified. The more we talked, the clearer things became; I realized that I had indeed been betrayed. The client didn't need me anymore: they had my engineering designs, my contacts, and my manufacturers. They had won.

They had all the leverage and held all the cards except for the remaining trailers full of my "defective" product, which they still wanted. All I held on to was my dignity and integrity. Unlike my opponents, I had acted honorably. Somehow, on that December day, that didn't seem to count for much.

I didn't tell them about my plans at the end of that meeting: I honestly didn't know what I was going to do. Extremely discouraged, I flew back to California, fired the East Coast law firm I had been working with, and hired another lawyer, a friend who had helped me establish my company years earlier.

Over the next few months, my company attempted to settle with the client. I was willing to cut my losses and take less than the original payment agreed upon. However, when I did not receive any response from the client, I moved forward with suing them on March 8, 2012. This date holds significance for me because of the other things that happened on that day, things of which I soon became aware.

The day I filed the lawsuit in California, I was in Hong Kong on business. Less than a mile away from my Hong Kong address, the client was busy negotiating with the Chinese manufacturer I had contracted to produce their product, who still held the remaining trailers of product. After paying off the manufacturer, the client absconded with multiple trailers of merchandise and, with it, every ounce of leverage I had. The product was worth a huge amount of money. While I could have sued the manufacturer for selling merchandise he did not own, I didn't have the time, energy, or money for another lawsuit. Instead, I decided to focus all my energy on recouping my losses from my original client.

In federal lawsuits, each party is required to attend mediation in hopes of settling the case without an expensive trial. In February 2013, both I and my client agreed to meet with a mediator, a retired judge recommended by the opposing counsel. The mediation involved three rooms: one for me and my counsel, one for the opposing party and their counsel, and one for both parties to come together and present their case before the mediator. Prior to the joint conference, we each adjourned to speak privately to our respective lawyers. Shortly thereafter, the mediating judge knocked and entered my room.

He had the nerve to say, "Sarah, why don't you walk away from this case? You are a foreigner in this country. The jury will look at you and instantly make up their minds. Your client has a popular product and a wholesome reputation. You are going to lose." He tried to force my hand and blackball me into giving up. It was a sneaky and underhanded maneuver! I was in shock, but I gathered my emotions and looked him straight in the eye. Mustering my courage, I said, "It's not all about me. I have many people depending on me to bring justice to this case. I have a family and employees whose futures are invested in this. I cannot walk away. I have no choice; I will keep fighting."

The judge saw that I was not deterred and changed tactics. He asked to speak privately to my lawyer, and they chatted outside the room for a long time. When my lawyer returned to the conference room, he looked shocked. He said the judge had offered him a job at the court if he talked me out of the lawsuit. The judge had tried another underhanded tactic, this time bribery, to manipulate me into surrendering.

I did not have time to react or confront the mediator. The judge called us back into the central room for the conference. After an hour, we had failed to reach a settlement. Before the judge left, he came to my room one last time and said, "Why don't you go home and ask your daddy and mommy about walking out of the case? Think seriously about it. You are a foreigner. You are going to lose."

As I considered the additional estimated $160,000 in legal fees to take the case to trial, and weighed that against the mediator's push to surrender, I came to the solid conviction that it was not hopeless. I was not going home, and I was not giving up. As the trial date drew closer, my lawyer had a second round of depositions, this time with the father (who held the test allegedly discrediting my product), Nancy, Dana (who had experience in marketing), and her soon-to-be ex-husband. I notified the family that I would fly out to the East Coast to meet them. Wow, did that get their attention!

By this time, their company, thanks in large part to the product I helped them create, was very successful both online and in stores around the country and abroad. It painted itself as a wholesome family company with a wholesome family product. The family did not want the publicity my lawsuit and trial would bring. One day before we were scheduled to meet, their lawyer contacted my lawyer with another settlement offer. Drained physically, mentally, emotionally, and especially financially, I desperately needed a decent settlement. I had even taken out a mortgage on my home. If I were to have any hope of resurrecting my business and my life, this was it!

Everything led up to this point. My whole family—my mother, brother, and sister—had been dragged into the situation, and it had taken its toll on everyone. For the sake of my family, I gave my lawyer a specific dollar amount I would consider in a settlement: I told him, "If they offer you this, take it, even though it isn't what I am owed." This number did not account for my personal time and anguish, but it was an amount I believed they were likely to accept.

I arrived on the East Coast ready to proceed with the deposition when I received the news from my lawyer: the case had been settled. I never again had to face the people who had caused me and my family so much grief. The drama was over, and all I felt was relief. However, it wasn't a victory.

About a year later, I began having a particular dream over and over again: in it, Danielle apologized to me repeatedly, saying, "I'm so sorry. I'm so sorry. I finally know how it feels to lose a father." These dreams made me curious, so I looked online for news about her father and found that he had passed away a few weeks earlier. I also read online that her sister, Dana, had filed for divorce. I began wondering if her marriage problems had something to do with the family's sudden interest in avoiding a deposition and jury trial. The news could have damaged the family's wholesome reputation and resulted in potentially adversarial, unflattering comments about the family business.

I thought back to Danielle's words in my dream and the trusting relationship we supposedly had. When my father died in 2010, she had sent a very heartwarming letter to my family and me: she wrote how sad she felt, because she knew my father was the backbone of our family. How did that relationship, that trust, turn into such an awful mess? It felt like a million years ago: so much had happened that destroyed our early good faith. As I pondered what went wrong, I realized a few important lessons.

LESSONS

1. Love of money is the root of all evil

Money is how I ended up in this situation. More specifically, the love of money. Let's not pretend that money isn't critical for anyone who creates, grows, and runs a small business. If you don't have or make money, you're not going to be in business for very long: running a business requires managing your money wisely.

But if your love of money is stronger than your love for people or stronger than your desire for respect earned from doing the right thing, then you will fail. Maybe not this quarter or this fiscal year—maybe not for decades to come—but eventually. As I learned in my dealings with this family, money, greed, and pride bring out the worst in people. I was misled, lied to, cheated, deceived, degraded, and humiliated, all for the love of money.

Today, I pause every time I enter a new relationship with a client or supplier and ask myself: Am I treating this person fairly? Am I treating this person honorably? Am I treating this person in the way I want to be treated?

2. Get it in writing

No matter who you're in business with, no matter how righteous or honest or Christian they appear, you need a solid contract. It's not cynical to require a contract; it's wise. A contract lays out all unspoken desires and expectations. No one is immune to greed or selfishness. No one.

3. Don't ignore your gut feelings

Some people call it discernment: a sense of warning to which you'd better respond or figure out the reason behind. When I learned Danielle was going on a solo vacation to Hong Kong, that was a warning. The odd sense my staff and I got from the COO was a warning. My phone and laptop dying was a warning. My former employee's name in the client's company email was a warning. It is important to pay attention to all warning signs, both obvious and subtle.

4. Don't be afraid to fight for justice

You may be an individual or a small company, but that does not mean you shouldn't fight for justice. Remind yourself of David and Goliath: David was a shepherd, not a skilled warrior like the giant Goliath, but God was on David's side. If you are on the side of justice, do not be afraid to fight, no matter how fierce the giants in your life appear.

If you are just starting your business, please do not assume that all business relationships are toxic. This story stands out precisely because it was so unexpected. The predominant number of my clients and suppliers are loyal and wonderful. Many started with me when I began my business and are still with me today.

Despite my legal battles, I honestly feel happy for the company and the fact that they found success. I had a part in starting their business. Today they are doing many good deeds, are involved in charity work, and give back to their community. However, I often pray that they will not repeat the same offense against others as against me.

I faced a challenging situation and prevailed. I never expected to end up in such an adversarial relationship with a unique client. I also never expected to deal with betrayal within my own company. Little did I know that these hardships would follow me as I searched for a new CEO.

5

HE LOOKED GOOD ON PAPER

By 2009, I became very concerned about my father's health as he progressively became more ill. I spent the majority of 2009 out of the California office and in Hong Kong, so I could be closer to my father and the rest of my family. Because of this, I was searching for someone to manage my company. I had several long-time employees, and we were doing well financially. We had several big clients and our business had grown to several million dollars a year. Everything was running smoothly enough that I was only working nine months out of the year. I thought the company was strong enough for me to consider bringing on an administrator, someone who could handle the business and free up my time so I could focus on my family and pursue other opportunities.

In October 2008, I received an email from a longtime friend saying, "Sarah, I met this guy at a Bible study whose name is Ernie. He's an international lawyer, business consultant, a citizen of Germany, and he has lived in Hong Kong for a long time. I thought it would be interesting for you guys to meet. Perhaps he can help you with your business!"

Over the years, this friend had set up several opportunities for me to meet people in my field; some could benefit my business and others needed my help with self-publishing. I trusted this friend and was intrigued enough to meet this guy. Little did I know that by 2012 I would be filing a restraining order against him.

It all started when I agreed to meet Ernie for lunch at a Chinese restaurant in Monterey Park. It was a professional meeting, but my friend had mentioned that this guy was single, and I have to admit there was a little bit of romantic tension at our meeting. He told me his whole life story over lunch, and it became obvious that his intention was to date me. He was very tall, 6-foot-3, not bad looking. He definitely seemed older than me, probably by about ten years. He also seemed remarkably intelligent, a trait I have always admired. He could talk about anything. He even knew some of my language, because he had worked in Hong Kong. However, I had a gut feeling that this relationship should stay professional.

At the time of our meeting, he was living in the dormitory of a local seminary and claimed to be a student there. However, as the conversation continued, I learned that he had been a student at the seminary for ten years but never graduated. He explained that he kept pushing his graduation date because he needed a student visa to legally stay in the United States. He also told me that even though he was living in a dorm, he owned a house in northern California close to one of the companies for which he did freelance consulting, and he regularly traveled back and forth between northern and southern California. A few details of his story seemed a little odd, but I believed him. He pitched himself as both a good catch romantically and as a great CEO candidate.

I needed a CEO, and this man wanted to be a CEO. What could go wrong? The CEO conversation was no coincidence.

6

SHEEP'S CLOTHING

I spent much of 2009 flying back and forth between Hong Kong and California, but I made time to go out to dinner several times with Ernie. Interestingly, when we ate out he expected me to pay the bill and pick him up, even though he had a car. I remember thinking that he conducted himself in an unusual way.

I hosted a big party at my house and invited Ernie along with twenty or so of my friends. After dinner, a few—some of my closest friends and confidantes—approached me. One told me, "Who is this guy? I don't like him; be careful, Sarah!" Another said, "I have extremely bad vibes about this guy."

My immediate response was that my friends were wrong. I felt like they were attacking him for no reason. I desperately wanted them to like him, and I didn't take their advice well. My ego and emotions were clouding my perspective and judgment.

I admired him. I thought, this guy has all these qualifications. He's very spiritual and seems to know a lot about the Bible, both traits that are extremely important to me. Because of my frequent travels to Hong Kong, we could only see each other sporadically. Therefore, we frequently talked on the phone for extended periods of time about all sorts of things. He had qualities I admired. Our relationship seemed to be going in the right direction, and we appeared to be a good match.

Then, in late 2009, Ernie surprised me by moving out of seminary housing and packing up his house in northern California to move to his other house in southern California, a house he had never told me about. But he explained that owning a few houses did not make him a rich man and confessed that he was having serious financial problems. With the economic recession, both of his houses were "upside down," and he owed more on the homes than they were now worth. He talked a lot about money and how he was struggling financially, as well as being in poor health. We also had many conversations where he asked me to donate large amounts of money to different organizations. Looking back, our conversations often centered on money.

As 2010 approached, my company was doing well, but my father was worse, and I was depressed. I was looking for a way out; hiring a CEO seemed like the best answer, and here was a guy with great qualifications right in front of me. I ignored all the warning signs, invited him to look at my business, and in March 2010, retained Ernie as a freelance consultant.

His first project with me was a trade show in northern California with two other employees. The trade show went well, and I assured myself that I had made a good choice. I flew back to Hong Kong later that month, and as I boarded the airplane I felt what I now believe to be a false sense of peace. Agonizing over my father's failing health, I needed all other aspects of my life to be in sync.

When I arrived in Hong Kong, my father was much worse than I expected; his health faded quickly. I stayed until he died at the end of March. The sorrow of his passing, details of the family business in Hong Kong, and my own depression led me to make a foolish decision: I contacted my California office and, over speaker phone, told the entire staff I was appointing Ernie as the interim CEO. I told them he would make decisions until I returned and gave him access to all of my financial data and almost everything I owned: my assets, QuickBooks, computers, personal office, and keys to my building. I had several million dollars of sales revenue that year, and he knew all the details.

While I remained in Hong Kong, he appeared supportive and caring on the phone. He said the right things and told me what I needed to hear. Emotionally, I trusted him to run the company. When he told me that he intended to revamp my business, starting with operations, I agreed: I was dealing with my father's funeral arrangements and in a very fragile emotional state. After all, this was why I hired him, wasn't it? The answer was: yes, he knew what he was doing, but it wasn't taking care of my company.

7

THE WOLF TURNS

When I finally came back to California after my father's funeral in April, my office looked very different. A lot of things—pictures, plants, some of the furniture, and fixtures—were gone, along with some of my personal items, many items from the warehouse, and some of our computer equipment. Ernie told me he had hired a handyman that morning, the morning of my arrival, to dispose of any items he felt unnecessary as part of the "revamp" of my operation. I couldn't believe that he would throw all my things away. There was a dumpster out back, but when I went to look, my items were not there. I wondered if they had been sold. If so, where had the money gone?

He had also promoted one of my employees. He had contacted me about this while I was away, and while I wasn't sure it was the best idea, in my stress and tiredness, I had reluctantly agreed. Now I had a marketing director, but another problem on my hands: two valued employees resigned immediately upon my return.

What happened during those weeks I was in Hong Kong? To this day, I do not know why those employees left. As I thought back to the smooth, convincing manner in which Ernie spoke, he could have persuaded my employees to believe anything. He was extremely talented at manipulation. In a matter of hours after my return, I became very angry and suspicious. I found paperwork for his freelance clients in the office trash can and, when I accessed his office computer, emails proving he had done business for others while supposedly revamping my company. One of my loyal employees confided, "Sarah, don't trust this man. While you were in Hong Kong, he kept his office door closed all the time." Well, for good reason! At least some of the time he was behind closed doors, he was working for someone else.

What kind of man was my new CEO? I should not have been surprised by what I discovered. As I delved deeper into his computer, I discovered he had been chatting online with different women. This didn't include a new girlfriend in SoCal and another woman in NorCal. His online history included visits to a site soliciting prostitutes and one-night stands and very explicit conversations. Signs of this behavior were evident in previous conversations we'd had on the topic of premarital intimacy; unfortunately, I chose not to believe these signifiers and was instead blinded to all but the qualities I wanted to see.

One of the online communications I uncovered was so secretive, it was humorous. When I made travel arrangements to see my father, Ernie had connected me to some of his Hong Kong friends. He then proceeded to share news about his intimate adventures, including a message which said something to the tune of, "I'm seeing this other woman. Don't tell Sarah!"

I thank God to this day that I only had a professional business relationship with this deceitful man. The warnings my friends had given me months before finally sank in. He played every angle to ensure that he covered his own bases. From what I saw, his entire life was a deception.

8

IT ENDS HERE. EXCEPT IT DOESN'T

I made the decision at the end of April 2010 to discharge Ernie in the middle of our conference room. I caught him completely by surprise: I did not tell him any of the things I had discovered, I simply fired him. He didn't argue, plead, or try to convince me to change my mind. Instead, he told me how much money I owed him. What?!

When I first brought him on as a consultant, he charged me almost $400 per hour, billing me at an attorney's rate. I was stupid enough to agree and to pay him regularly. Now he claimed I still owed him $50,000 of overtime for the one month he worked as CEO. This included, he said, the 20 hours he spent researching and referring doctors to help with my father's treatment (and yes, he did refer us to one doctor, who we never used). He had no records to confirm this overtime, but that didn't stop him from demanding these funds.

I refused. I had the accounting record detailing his payment while he was working for other people. However, I still wanted a clean break, so I reminded him of an occasion when he used his legal expertise to help settle an international dispute in his role as consultant. At the time, I had agreed to give him a $30,000 lump sum from the settlement money as compensation. Now, I told him, "I'm terminating you, but I'll give you that $30,000 lump sum right now. In exchange, you must sign a release form that says I don't owe you anything. I just want you to get out of my company."

Ernie agreed to my terms and signed the release. He then later claimed the release form was not binding, since he had signed it under duress and because of my emotional distress. Later, when I attended law school, I found his statement to be an amusing tactical twist, as if his consent was invalid because of my distress.

I gave him the $30,000 and believed we were free of him. Yet, he would not go away that easily. He still believed I owed him $50,000 in overtime, and I began to feel like I was being stalked. He tried to reach me through repeated emails and texts every month. Over and over he would tell me, "When are you going to pay me? You still owe me money. We're Christians; we're supposed to deal with this in a Christian way." He had seen my full financial statements and assumed I could afford to pay him.

This behavior went on for a couple of years, and then he made a serious mistake. His emails and texts began to refer to my father's death: "If your father hadn't died, I wouldn't have spent so much time helping you. I spent a lot of my personal time keeping your company afloat after you were shattered by your father's death." It made me furious that he was using my father's death to get money from me. I dug in my heels.

In August 2012, I filed a restraining order against my ex-CEO. We went to court in Rancho Cucamonga, California, and he brought my former marketing director, the employee promoted in my absence, as his character witness. The marketing director wrote in his affidavit that my ex-CEO was his mentor, even though he had worked in the office for only one month and apparently had his door closed the entire time. The marketing director claimed he was a wonderful man, the man he respected most in the world. There were also letters the CEO had culled from former employee and from one of the employees who resigned after my return, all discrediting me.

One of those letters is worth mentioning further. My heart was aggrieved when she submitted this letter to the court, because it was by a young woman whose mother is in a Bible study group with me and a good friend. This young lady was released from my employment because she was inappropriately using company time. I assumed this was an opportunity for her to get revenge and humiliate me. I could not bring myself to read the letter more than once. A few years later, her mother told me her daughter regretted writing the letter. She began having serious health issues and believed God was punishing her for lying. She asked me for forgiveness, which I granted.

Back in court, much to my dismay, the paperwork for the restraining order was not completed correctly, and the judge did not grant my request. Yet, she did something else amazing: she grilled my former CEO in court, telling him not to contact me or to send me any more emails. She warned him that if he continued his behavior, she would make sure I got a restraining order that was vigorously enforced. The lecture got his attention, and he did not contact me again. Believe it or not, however, he was still not out of my life.

LESSONS

1. Wolves are real

After this was all over, I told my mom, "I'm so glad I went through this ordeal because I learned from it. It was an eye-opening experience: 'Welcome to the real world, Sarah!'" I don't know what you have been through, but I never thought this kind of thing would happen to me. I am living proof that this isn't something that only happens in books, movies, or TV. This is real life, and there are people who are out to deceive, trick, and manipulate you to achieve their own agendas. They are true wolves disguised in sheep's clothing. A special warning to this end: Whether you are married or single, rich or poor, and especially if you have some financial means, do not disclose your financial information to anyone other than your personal accountant.

2. Keep professional relationships professional

While I was not in a romantic relationship with this man, the possibility was always there. If we had been romantically entangled, it would have made things even worse. The dynamics of a business relationship are much different than those of a romantic one. If you start mixing the two, you'll likely be unsuccessful in both.

3. Don't make decisions when you're grieving

This might be common sense, but I didn't follow this piece of advice. I made a life-changing business decision at a time when I was depressed, discouraged, distressed, distracted, and distraught. I hired someone to run my company and then gave him the keys. Looking back, I must have been out of my mind. At the time, though, I would have defended my decision. This underscores the importance of surrounding yourself with wise counselors, friends, or elders. This is essential not just for a small business, but in life. There will be times when you are turned upside down and inside out, and you'll struggle to think straight and make wise decisions. You will need people to whom you can turn to for advice and counsel.

4. Don't lose the keys

As a business owner, don't let someone else run your business. You must maintain final authority and responsibility over your organization and product. If you do not, you may lose not only inventory from your warehouse or dollars from your balance sheet, but also the hearts of your employees. This doesn't mean that you must be the only manager in the company or personally oversee all daily business. It does, however, mean that you should never allow your company to lose the sense that you're in charge, making final decisions, and setting company standards and values.

5. Pay attention to the instincts of those who care about you

In an earlier chapter I described the importance of paying attention to your instincts or gut feelings. You should also listen to the people who love you. They can often see things from different angles, especially when you are blinded by your own pride or passion. Take your friends' warnings seriously, even if you don't like what you hear.

Use discretion and seek counsel from two or more trusted friends. Remember, I met Ernie because he was introduced to me by a friend, a university professor who had no idea about his behavior. Be wise and listen and seek wisdom from more than one person who has your best interest in mind.

6. Be cautious, not afraid

Draw the right lessons from my stories, not the wrong ones. I don't want you to read this book and think, *Wow, I can never trust anybody, or I must be hard and protect myself so that nobody knows the real me.* If you're thinking about starting a small business, don't back out because you are fearful and think, *Oh, I shouldn't do this. All these awful things will happen to me! It'll be horrible!*

In the life of a small business, just like in general, there will be difficult decisions, decisions that don't seem clear or black and white. There will be times when a decision looks like a great opportunity and will involve terrifying risk. Don't be afraid. At those times, you will need counsel from wise colleagues and leaders, elders and mentors, and family and friends. You will need to lean on wisdom bigger than your ego and emotions, deeper than your circumstances, and stronger than the storms you will sail into.

To be independent of the fear, ego, emotions, circumstances, and storms, yet dependent on wisdom, is how to live a life that is positive and that perseveres.

9

SARAH: AMERICA'S MOST WANTED

By late 2012, I thought I had Mr. CEO out of my life, but I was wrong. In October 2012, two months after the court hearing about my restraining order, I received a letter from the IRS saying that they intended to audit my tax returns. I was troubled, but not shocked: small businesses get audited from time to time. The one bit of information that bothered me was their desire to audit my returns from 2010: the notification seemed unusual. Why that year? Why not 2007, when we were doing more business and made a couple of million more in revenue than in 2010? Why not 2008 or 2011? It turns out that 2010 was the year my ex-CEO worked in the office.

My lawyers suspected that my former CEO had portrayed himself to the IRS as some sort of "whistleblower" and that this was why the IRS was interested in this year. Ernie had access to all my financial information while he was in the office, including my financial statements and QuickBooks. He knew there were millions of dollars of revenue coming through my account and of my operations in Hong Kong and China. Besides my CPA, he was the only person who had inside information about my U.S. and overseas operations.

The IRS auditor let slip a clue: when my CPA met with the auditor for the first time, we assumed she would ask questions about my taxes, even though the initial letter from the IRS was vague. However, the first words out of her mouth were a different kind of tactical question: "What if I discovered that Sarah has been committing fraud?"

10

IT GETS WORSE

I was stunned to realize this was not an investigation of tax issues or financial irregularities. It became obvious that an allegation of fraud had been made against me. As to who had made the allegation, the clues pointed to the one person with access to my finances and with a motive to plant such an allegation. Someone who knew enough about my international business dealings to know the exact words that would gain the IRS' attention. I, my lawyer, and my CPA all had our suspicions: my former CEO had fired one last poison dart and aimed it with pointed accuracy.

The year 2013 became a blizzard of paper. I confess I was not an organized person when it came to receipts, statements, and invoices, but I did keep everything, and this became my salvation. There may not have been a clear system, but everything I needed was there. More than one staff member had asked me, "Why do you keep all these old receipts and bills?" But even if I didn't know how to efficiently organize them, I knew they were important. We're not talking about a few dozen pieces of paper, or even a couple of hundred: I had thousands of receipts, invoices, bills, and statements. I held on to every last receipt, and these were available when the IRS requested them.

In late 2013, one year into the investigation, my lead lawyer and I met the auditor at the IRS headquarters in San Bernardino, California. Fraud wasn't the only accusation I heard at this meeting: the IRS added money laundering to the investigation. Money laundering! The term immediately brings up images of drug cartels and organized crime. During criminal investigations, investigators "follow the money." Money laundering is when large amounts of dirty money that comes from illegal activities, such as drug trafficking or terrorist groups, are funneled through a legitimate business. The term describes the operation to a tee: it's like washing laundry to clean what is dirty. Dirty money looks clean and is difficult for investigators to find.

The auditor questioned why I did not report as income several thousand dollars deposited into my account in April 2010. She found this suspicious and inquired if I had been funneling money from some undisclosed source. I explained that this was not income, but a series of financial gifts for my father's funeral expenses. In Chinese culture, funeral guests bring money in white envelopes for the family of the deceased. These can be directly addressed to a family member or put in a donation box. If a person is unable to attend the funeral, it is appropriate to mail a monetary gift to the family. The money is a sign of respect for the deceased and for the family and is to be used to assist with funeral expenses.

I further explained that the amount given varies depending on the deceased's family income and that of the guests. It also depends on how close the guest is to the grieving family. Tradition specifies that the amount should be in multiples of $100 HK plus $1 HK, as the amount must always be an odd number. The minimum that is considered appropriate is $101 HK, or about $13 US, but there is no upper limit. Gifts may be anonymous, but usually an individual signs their name so that the family receiving the money will later reciprocate and give the same amount to the guest upon the future death of their loved one.

In my situation, my father and family were deeply respected in Hong Kong, and the gifts were generous. I managed the details of my father's funeral and estate, so it was my responsibility to record the amounts given. As the gift givers expect reciprocation, these records are important. I processed all the gifts and deposited them as individual entries into my account. I then transferred them, again as individual entries, into my mother's account. I could see how, from the IRS' point of view, this activity seemed suspicious. But they were simply gifts, not personal income and certainly not money laundering. Each gift was transferred, dollar for dollar, to my mother on whatever day they were received.

I requested that my mother FedEx me her bank account information. She is old-school, and there is nothing digital about her accounting system. She keeps paper bankbooks, and that is what I received via FedEx. I opened my mother's tattered old bankbooks and told the auditor, "Right here, you can see years and years of records of my mother's bank account. You can see the handwritten logs of the deposited gifts." Even though the auditor said she didn't need to see it, I made a copy. I wanted to clearly show the money going in and out on the same day, proving there was no increase in my own personal account.

This is only one of many times I was requested to substantiate claims and then told, "Oh, I don't need that" when I presented evidence. I felt like a criminal and that I was being treated like one. Every time I was asked to explain, prove with documentation, or substantiate a claim in any way, it felt like an accusation. The IRS was accusing me of committing fraud, hiding income, and knowingly filing false tax returns. It was gut-wrenching, because I knew the source of the money and the reason behind the paperwork. To talk about the funeral gifts and to see the familiar, careful handwriting in my mother's bankbooks made this particular session with the auditor a difficult day for me. Yet it was even harder when I needed to present evidence that my father had died. The specificity of the request broke me: my professional presence, my self-control, and my never-give-in facade all crumbled, and I began to sob. I handed the auditor my father's death certificate with trembling fingers and tears streaming down my face.

11

IT GETS BETTER

When I handed over my father's death certificate, my lawyer became angry at the auditor. He barked at her, "There's obviously no criminal activity here! What are you fishing for? Does this have to do with my former CEO? Because I can tell you some things about that guy!" At the mention of my former CEO, the auditor looked away. She handed me a box of tissues and sat back in her chair. At that moment, something changed. I don't know if it came from her mind or her heart, but I had the distinct feeling that a darkness had lifted. Things felt less oppressive, even though the ordeal was still far from over.

After failing to find anything fraudulent in my 2010 transactions, the IRS sent me a letter in early 2014 telling me that my 2011 tax returns would also be audited. When the government starts an investigation, they will pursue it until they find something. If they put the time and effort into an audit, they won't give up easily. It is like going out in a boat and not coming back to shore until one catches at least one fish.

I spent much of 2014 in the same exhausting process of providing documentation for every single transaction I had made in 2011. As I mentioned earlier, 2011 was the year of my dispute with my East Coast client, along with other issues. Most of my financial paperwork remained unorganized, but I managed to pull together what the IRS needed. I substantiated my income and expenditures down to the penny.

I collected and presented the IRS with 10,000 documents, including statements of all my credit card accounts and receipts from China and Hong Kong. When my representative met with the auditor, the auditor told her, "Oh I don't need that"; we gave it to her anyway. I flew to Hong Kong for two days to collect documentation, including several necessary bank documents that could not be released without in-person proof of identification. The bank had to print each document at a cost of $10 per document. It was extremely frustrating to have to spend time chasing down documentation instead of focusing on my business. But it worked! When I presented the auditor with the second mountain of paperwork proving I had nothing to hide, she seemed convinced I was not involved in any malicious criminal activity.

In early 2015, I had a hearing in front of a judge. While the criminal accusations had finally been put to rest, this hearing addressed whether I had tax irregularities and liabilities that needed correcting. The auditor and her supervisor, the regional manager, attended the hearing. While it was not held in a regular courtroom, it still caused me some anxiety. However, I quickly surmised that I had nothing to be anxious about; the judge was friendly and put me at ease with small talk. I wonder now if he was trying to get a sense of my character, of who I was as a person. His wife was Chinese, and we talked about some of the places he had visited in China.

The meeting soon turned technical. My representative, the auditor, and the judge began to review certain transactions from 2010 and 2011 to determine if I had additional tax liabilities or corrections. The issues seemed to revolve around timing, such as whether I had claimed certain transactions during the correct tax year. The final result was the imposition of minor interest payments and penalties, with which I did not disagree.

The auditor, however, doggedly remained on my case. Although there were no criminal misdeeds, for unknown reasons she wanted to continue the audit. Her supervisor and the judge both asked her several times to close the case. The judge even raised the possibility of potential liability for the IRS, reminding her that I could turn around and sue the agency. Her supervisor told her that the ordeal had gone on too long: she had found nothing significant, and it was time to conclude the audit. Finally, she reluctantly agreed to stop. After three long years, it was finally over. I even received a verbal apology from two upper-level IRS officials. How often do you imagine that happens? To me, this made up for all the hours of tracking down documents and the money spent on attorneys. I had settled the issue, and my lead tax attorney deserved the extremely heartfelt thanks I bestowed upon him. I breathed a sigh of relief.

LESSONS

What lessons can be learned from an IRS audit, other than to hope and pray it never happens to you? I gleaned a few things from this experience.

1. Don't panic

An audit doesn't convict you of anything; the IRS is just looking. But let's be honest, it's a lot easier to avoid panic if you've followed my other lessons below.

2. Maintain a good reputation

I believe that one of the things that helped me with the IRS auditor was that I had a clean record. I had no history of shady dealings, scandals, or trouble, and I did not have to explain any past irregularities or questionable practices. My lawyers also had good reputations: their integrity and experience gave them instant credibility. We went into this investigation with nothing to hide and nothing to apologize for, and I was cleared.

3. Have documentation and evidence

Even though the law in the United States is "innocent until proven guilty," I very much felt the burden of proof. The only way to supply such proof is through documentation, not with pleading or arguing. When the IRS raised a question, I needed to provide an answer with a legitimate paper trail. I don't think my pleas of innocence would have gone very far without the mountains of papers I brought along with me.

4. Be organized

Having the necessary documentation won't help you if you can't find it. As a small business owner, it is tempting to spend all your time doing what you love and not doing the boring administrative work. If you own a candle shop, you want to spend your time designing, making, and selling candles, not filing receipts. If you're a publisher like me, you'd rather come up with new book designs and help your authors instead of managing invoices and statements. But though many of us may be artists, we are also business people, which means that things have to be done in an efficient, effective way. For me, this meant that I had to organize my financial paperwork. I had to develop a system of filing and tracking all my documents. I would have saved myself hours of work (and stress!) if I had that system in place before I was audited. Even if you have an accountant on staff, check on them and their system. You must know and understand this aspect of your business. If you don't have an accountant, it's up to you. Get it done and do it well.

12

THE WORM STORY

I already mentioned the art director who called me a "worm." This conversation occurred in mid-October 2012, just a few weeks before I received the IRS letter launching years of investigations.

As I said, refusing to work with that art director meant walking away from a substantial book deal with a major airline and perhaps future work with New York firms.

There were many times during the IRS investigation when I was writing a number of large checks to lawyers. So much money was being dispersed, so much of my life was consumed by legal issues that I didn't have time to drum up new business especially when I could have benefited from money coming in. More than a few times I wondered if giving up that deal was such a smart thing to do. Maybe I should have just swallowed his insults and continued working with him: I would have received a substantial amount of money.

But I didn't ruminate on these things for long. In my heart I knew I had done the right thing, even if it was at a cost. This is often the case: doing the right thing comes at a cost and you must decide if you are willing to pay it. My experience has taught me that the cost of not doing the right thing comes with an even higher price to pay. Indeed, this story taught me some important lessons that have formed the bedrock of my life since then.

LESSONS

1. You will face more than one challenge at a time: Be prepared

We often hear people complain that it's just one thing after another or when it rains, it pours. I realized that multiple tough things may happen at the same time, even in a small business. You cannot become so consumed by one challenge that you stop paying attention to everything else. If dealing with the airline book project had consumed me with disappointment and frustration, I might have tossed that IRS letter into a drawer instead of taking it seriously.

2. When people punch you, you don't have to punch back

Respond to insult with dignity and character to ensure your words and actions reflect who you are. In this case, I chose to confront the art director, not by calling him names but by telling him politely and firmly that he was being insulting. I wanted to let him know the consequences of his actions; namely, that I wasn't going to work with him any longer.

3. Pay attention to character

This man never apologized, including during the multiple attempts he later made to contact me. For me, that became an issue of character and I had no interest in doing business with that kind of person. You do not need to partner with people who do not respect you. If you do, it will lead to regret and multiple problems down the road.

If the art director had apologized, would I have gone back and worked with him? Perhaps, but with my eyes wide open. Someone who does not respect you now will likely not respect you later. You set yourself up for continuing problems if you choose to work with someone who is disrespectful. Those problems may cost time, money, emotional energy, and aggravation.

4. Stand your ground and know your worth

Know your worth and where you stand. Never compromise your standards even if short on revenue. This will pay off in the long run. Focus on pursuing accounts and customers who respect and value you and who are willing to partner with you for the long haul.

This incident impressed upon me that no matter the size of the business, we can and must be selective with whom we choose to work, according to our company's own standards. Today, seven years later, my business is much better than it would have been had I dealt with this art director. Imagine the distress and extra resources he would have consumed. You don't have to deal with the drama of someone like that: it's not worth it.

It's important to set those standards early on, when your business is still small. If you wait until a big opportunity comes along, it will be too late. Without establishing standards or principles, it is far too easy to compromise when "big money" is suddenly presented and you're tempted to grab the money and worry about the principles later.

13

STUCK IN NEW JERSEY

The month of May brings joy for students because the school year is finishing, and summer vacation is around the corner. But for publishers like me it is a month of stress and tight deadlines. In 2013, my company signed a contract to provide yearbooks to several schools in the New York/New Jersey area. One of my employees handled the logistics of transporting the yearbooks across the country from California and contracted with a large, well-known trucking company to handle transportation and delivery.

The 2013 school schedule coincided closely with the Memorial Day holiday weekend, which meant that our transportation had to take place in a tight window of time. The trucking company picked up the books and started the cross-country trip to New Jersey. However, on the day they were supposed to pick up the load, they went to the wrong location, 50 miles off course. I knew straightening out this situation would cost me a full day and, if we lost a day to transport the yearbooks, we might not be able to deliver them on time. I felt an ominous sensation: things were going to end badly. Little did I know that this was only the beginning of my problems.

My highest priority was to deliver the yearbooks on time. I directed my employee to cancel the contract with the trucking company and hire another, regardless of cost. The new company offered guaranteed delivery, which I agreed to pay for, and their rates were three times higher than the first company. But when this new company arrived to pick up the freight, the dock was empty. The first trucking company had arrived earlier in the day and picked up the freight. Because the warehouse had not received the message about hiring a new trucking company, they released the product.

After we realized this, we told the first company to turn around and release the freight to the new trucking company. They refused to do so, claiming they held a two-hour lead and had already traveled outside of the area. I didn't know if this was true and I had no way of confirming. To put my mind at ease, both the dispatcher and sales representative verbally promised they'd provide free guaranteed delivery, just like the second company. After hearing this, I agreed to their terms and assumed everything would be okay.

However, something told me I still needed to follow up. So I checked in every single day, tracking the delivery from California to New Jersey and making sure it proceeded with the planned route and schedule. But when the yearbooks were supposed to arrive in New Jersey, the website indicated no movement or update. I started to panic! Where were they? What had happened to my yearbooks? I was about to get a lesson in the intricate business of interstate trucking.

14

WHERE ARE MY BOOKS?

The first trucking company decided to lease out my shipment to another company at some point in the transportation process. It took quite an effort on my end to figure out who hauled the books. When I tried to contact the affiliate trucking company who was now handling my merchandise, initially the customer service department in their Chicago office did not want to speak with me, because technically I was not their client. However, after over an hour of discussion and persistent pressure about the yearbooks' urgent delivery date, I discovered a shocking revelation: the original company never ordered guaranteed service when hiring the subcontractor. Because of this, the yearbooks were being transported at a normal, lower priority pace.

The first company misled me and never informed me of the changes. The subcontractor explained that if I wanted the books delivered earlier, I would be required to pay an expediting fee at 100% mark-up. Stuck between a rock and a hard place, I agreed. The Chicago-based subcontractor insisted I approve the change in writing and required that I get the original trucking company involved again. However, their office in California had not yet opened for the day.

No longer a matter of days, my deadline was now in hours; even an hour-long delay waiting for an office to open would be very costly. After finally connecting with the California-based company, I reluctantly gave my approval to the additional fees, telling them, "I have no choice but to agree to this, because you have my shipment. I agree to pay the extra expediting fee even though you had promised me there would be no extra fees." After committing to pay them twice as much as my original contract, the company agreed to expedite my yearbook delivery.

By the time my approval was conveyed from California to Chicago to the truckers, it was afternoon in New Jersey, and the trucks had to wait for the next morning to deliver. The next day, heavy traffic plagued New Jersey, and they were unable to deliver yet again. It wasn't until the following day, two days after the planned delivery, that the yearbooks arrived at the schools. Such a substantial delay of a hard deadline project is one of the worst things that can happen to a small business.

This unfortunate situation put a devastating dent in my business. Projects such as this are usually landed through a broker, who finds publishers such as mine on behalf of schools and districts. I was not selling books directly but through a wholesale service. The broker with whom I was working was concerned not only about this delivery, but about my trustworthiness for future deliveries. Although we had done business together for two years, he eliminated my company from any future business in the larger New Jersey / New York market.

It was also simply heartbreaking to know that students did not receive their books in a timely manner. By the time the books finally arrived, in early June, several of the schools were already closed for the summer.

One particular email from the broker still haunts me today: "You could just imagine how disappointed the students were when you looked at their faces, that they missed the opportunity, especially the graduating seniors . . . they missed the opportunity to have their friends sign a yearbook before they said goodbye." His disappointment was palpable, and he emotionally identified with the disappointed students. I completely understood their anguish too.

The broker said that he didn't blame me and knew I had tried my best to deliver the yearbooks on time. I reported daily updates as the freight moved from California, yet he still chose to cancel all future contracts, including those I had already contracted for the subsequent year. This amounted to a large business loss. He never returned as a client, even though I tried countless times to reinitiate our connection.

15

THE LAWSUIT THAT
SHOULDN'T HAVE BEEN

The bill from the trucking company did not come until August, and it was not what I expected. I was already unhappy about paying for expedited shipping when the service had been promised for free, not to mention the fact that the product had arrived late. But it turns out there was another issue: this time with the weight of the freight. A trucking company uses the shipment's weight as part of their calculation in figuring out how much to charge a customer. I knew the weight of my shipment, and the company was charging twice what I should have been owed. I spoke to the trucking company's CFO and had him investigate the expediting fee, the weight issue, and the delay in shipment. I asked him, "What are you going to do about this situation? We canceled the freight, and you took it anyway, despite the cancellation. You refused to turn around and subsequently agreed to expedited service for no charge, but never requested it from your subcontractor. When the freight finally arrived in New Jersey, your subcontractor and your company made me agree to pay double for expediting!" I expressed to him my frustration over the loss of substantial business and how my client had canceled all future business connections.

The CFO appeared to be an understanding man; he listened attentively to my detailed account. To protect myself, I included one of my employees and my secretary on the conference call. The CFO and his assistant also took part. By the end of the conversation, the CFO agreed to compensate us $10,000. I requested only $5,000, plus a waiver for the invoice. He agreed.

But then, in September, I received a collection letter from the trucking company stating, "If you don't pay the invoice we sent, we will sue you. We will take you to collections, and you'll be responsible for all legal fees." When I went back to the CFO, he totally disregarded everything he had previously stated about adjusting for the weight discrepancy and expediting fee and awarding compensation due to our loss of business. It was as if the previous phone conversation had never happened. He refused to respond to any emails, and I continued to receive demanding letters.

The invoice was only for $2,900, but I still felt angry. I was unwilling to pay for something that felt so wrong and that I didn't believe I owed. The trucking company continued to pursue its claim, adding continuous pressure. By the time my anger subsided, and my perspective became clearer, I told my lawyer that I wanted to settle. My instincts, law school experience, and understanding of the business world told me that this was the best choice. However, my lawyer disagreed and said we shouldn't pay. Out of respect for him, I chose not to pay any part of the invoice, not even the portion I agreed to. That was my first mistake.

The trucking company was unwilling to yield: they firmly stood their ground, requesting that we settle the invoice despite their mistakes. I paid my lawyer to analyze the case and to determine our chances of winning should we go to court. After reviewing my documentation, he affirmed that our evidence would yield a positive result. There was a compelling case: current business lost, future business lost, proof of multiple problems with delivery, my strong proactivity in tracking the shipment, absolute confirmation that I had notified the company of the delivery problems, and cancellation of the contract. We proceeded with the lawsuit, filing paperwork in the Los Angeles Superior Court in October 2013.

16

YOU WANT ME TO PAY WHAT?

I should have never filed this lawsuit, but I did. My lawyer had recently collected over $170,000 in fees during the legal dispute with my big East Coast client, and I suspected he thought, "You know, Sarah just collected some money; she has money in the bank." He knew the value of the settlement I received, and I firmly believe that his greed was a factor in this case.

The case against the trucking company continued to linger without any action or decisions through March 2015. Time went by with no response from the trucking company, and the court granted them an extension due to their slow response. Filing the necessary paperwork completely consumed 2014, yet my lawyer's legal fees were the only markers of progress. Delays also hinged on which court had the authority to rule over the lawsuit and whether the case would be a federal court case (since it involved interstate commerce) or a California state superior court case.

Finally, in March 2015, I presented my testimony in front of a judge at a scheduled court hearing at the Superior Court of California in Los Angeles. This was not a large multimillion-dollar case as in the lawsuit between my East Coast client and me: this was a simple bench trial with no jury and one judge who listened to the facts and made a verdict. The judge listened to both sides and issued his ruling a week later.

His final ruling was that I owed $2,900 to the trucking company; this was the amount I would have paid the company prior to filing a lawsuit. The dispute about the shipment's weight issue was never resolved, because my lawyer failed to raise the issue in court. The judge made his ruling based on the numbers in front of him.

The case should have been closed. However, a month after the ruling, the trucking company filed a motion claiming they spent $134,000 in legal fees and suing me for the costs. I had suspected this might happen. Their lawyer approached mine before the hearing, expressing the company's dissatisfaction at spending $134,000 in legal fees to collect $2,900. He offered to accept $72,000 for the fees and drop the motion for me to pay the full amount.

How could the company justify spending $134,000 in legal fees over the collection of a $2,900 debt? How much of that much money was actual legal fees? Court proceedings always include lapses of time when it seems like the case is going nowhere. True to form, from April to November 2015, there were stacks of papers passed back and forth between our lawyers, but nothing else happened. There is an old saying: "The wheels of justice turn slowly." Yes, they do. Very slowly. I was aware of this, yet I continued to write checks to my lawyer.

November 2015 finally brought another court hearing. Again, the judge ruled in favor of the trucking company, ruling that I owed $72,000, plus the original $2,900. I now owed almost $75,000 to a company that had failed to keep their promises and ended up costing me business while marring my reputation. I was astounded.

17

FIGHTING BACK

I often wonder if the trucking company saw me as a woman, member of an ethnic minority, and immigrant and decided there was an easy fix to this case. Did they surmise that because of these attributes I'd be a pushover? The trucking company originally wanted $134,000 but ended up asking for $72,000. According to an "Alice-in-Wonderland down-the-rabbit-hole" logic, this seems like a reasonable compromise: it's just over half the original demand. Once the judge pronounced this decision from the bench, I was forced to obey.

When a court makes a ruling, the judge must write an opinion about the case, explaining why he or she reached the decision. I asked several lawyers to review the opinion for this case, and they all suspected the judge had one of his law clerks prepare the opinion. This worked in our favor: the rationale was weak and the arguments were poorly written. I thought we might be able to have the decision reversed.

After we lost the ruling in March, my attorney almost disappeared. Meanwhile, he took the liberty of retaining one of his friends to represent me while we were still in lower court. Suddenly, one of his buddies, a man

I'd never met before, was representing me. This man also sent me bills for his work. My impressions and communication with this new lawyer gave me the sense that money was all he was concerned about. "When did you deposit that money into my account? Why did you not pay me yesterday?" Every email from him was about money. I felt decidedly uncomfortable about this "buddy" of my original attorney who had been retained without my approval.

When the court decided in November that I owed the trucking company $72,000, part of me was not surprised; legal representation will make or break a court case. Clear and concise representation is everything, and this new guy did not present himself in such a manner. It may sound unfair, but if the judge does not like your lawyer, it will screw up your case. I now faced the harsh reality of owing an additional $72,000 to a company that had cost me perhaps hundreds of thousands of dollars in long-term business.

As the day drew to a close, I gathered my emotions and surveyed my options. I had no money to pay this fee. I needed to choose: close the business, file for bankruptcy, or fight. To fight, I needed to appeal the case. But where would I find the money for attorney fees? I didn't have any answers. I had just finished a long-term legal dispute with my East Coast client and, with the ink barely dry on that settlement, I was now involved in another big case that could potentially shut down my company. Considering these circumstances, I strongly felt I had to appeal.

I had a one-month window to notify the court whether I would pay the $72,000 or appeal, and I started doing my own legal research. When an appeal is filed in a case with a potential judgment against you,

you must pay a bond. For example, the judgment was $72,000, so I had to present $72,000 as bond to be held in an escrow account. If I lost the case in appellate court, the $72,000 would transfer from the escrow account to the winning party. In other words, even if I appealed I needed to produce $72,000. I was in trouble.

I dug deeper in an attempt to clearly understand my responsibilities. I discovered that the bond requirement did not apply to me because my case concerned a judgment for legal fees. To protect public interest, legal fees are not included as part of a bond due to the controversy and contention surrounding them and to prevent an increase of greed among attorneys. I verified this exemption with ten different law firms to be certain my findings were correct.

Relieved, I temporarily stopped focusing on my immediate need for cash and concentrated on my appeal. Thanksgiving loomed on the horizon as I scrambled to contact and interview new law firms. Nine out of the ten I interviewed did not give me positive news about my chances. Even with the bench judge's shaky rationale, only one law firm was confident I could prevail. Several bluntly stated, "You may pay us, but there's a strong chance you will not win." One of the legal firms, one of the biggest firms in Los Angeles, would charge $70,000 in legal fees: the lawyer wanted me to pay that on top of my $72,000 judgment with no guarantee of winning. However, one small firm, with only two lawyers, caught my attention. As corny as it sounds, one word on the firm's website caught my eye, and I grabbed on to it as if it were my lifeline. The word: Justice.

18

AN ANGEL ON THE BENCH?

It would be worth every penny I owned if my new lawyer got justice on my behalf. I paid him to analyze the lower court's bench decision and was impressed when he responded not only in a timely manner, but also directly, not through a secretary or assistant. His first reaction could only be described as anger: anger on my behalf about the negligent and unjust decision. In addition to the court's opinion, I also showed him other court papers. He spent several hours personally reviewing them, after which he told me, "Sarah, you've got to fight this." He charged less than $400 to review my case and $7,000 to handle the entire appeal.

With only a few days to spare before the appeal deadline, I filed court papers at the appellate court to officially notify the court and opposing party's attorney of my intention to appeal. By now it was early January 2016. My new attorney busied himself filing paperwork at the appellate court, while I continued my business. As usual, this was a hectic time of year for my yearbook business. I did not actively follow up with the lawyer, because I trusted his expertise.

A key document in appellate court is the opening brief, a brief summary advising the court of why you believe the lower court made an incorrect decision. This opening brief lays the foundation of your legal arguments during a hearing. You cannot raise any new arguments during the hearing that are not included in this brief; so much weight rests on its strength. As important as this document was, however, I did not take the time to read through it before my new attorney submitted the brief to the court. I told myself I was too busy. It was an excuse and a costly mistake.

In spring 2016, several months later, I finally managed to read through this important document, weeks after it was filed. To my dismay, I discovered an error: a missing key argument. I became consumed by researching how to raise a new argument—one not included in the opening brief—at a hearing. The findings were definitely not in my favor: as expected, the bottom line is that you're not supposed to raise new arguments at a court hearing. Period. The court hearing brings clarity and additional detail to the already submitted opening brief.

When our appeal came to trial in December, I accompanied my attorney to court. There were five justices on the bench, and it was a solemn, cold environment. I warned my attorney, "You're going to be grilled. Be prepared! You must raise the argument you missed in the opening brief!" To his credit, he brought it up. As we both expected, he was thoroughly filleted and lambasted by several of the judges. I had researched the judges on the panel and suspected we would have trouble with some of them. But the lawyer's interrogation was not the case's turning point. Rather, the turning point happened because of the presence of a senior judge.

A senior judge is retired and offers to serve part-time if the current judges have too many cases. This senior judge, as it turns out, was not only experienced but also a presiding justice, or a judge who supervises a whole courthouse or judicial district. That day he was in charge of our case. This guardian angel of a man, after hearing arguments from both sides, stood up from the bench, looked at the other judges on the panel, and did something amazingly simple and clear. He reminded everyone that my contract with the trucking company had been canceled: "There is no contract!" he said. He then repeated the same phrase again: "There… is…no…contract!" The legal clause that allowed the trucking company to charge me for their legal fees was part of the contract. But if there wasn't a contract, they did not have any authority to charge me. Wow! This was the turning point: we knew we had won. The incomplete opening brief didn't matter. I had spent several weeks worrying for nothing. All along, God had a plan and was on my side the entire time.

Finally, someone heard me and stood up for me. I firmly believe God used this man, an 83-year-old retired presiding justice, to act on my behalf. He wrote the court opinion himself, including his rationale for the ruling. Normally the official ruling takes four months to be granted. But in my case, just one week later, close to Christmas, I received the official news that the appellate court had unanimously reversed the previous judgment. It was the most wonderful Christmas present. The judge even included a refund to me for court costs, which amounted to several thousand dollars.

In hindsight, although the yearbook broker in New Jersey will no longer conduct business with me, I am grateful that my business remained intact and that this ordeal did not bankrupt me. The experience gave me a renewed sense of God's blessing and touch on my life. It reminded me that God cares for me. These new lessons, learned the hard way, have had a lasting impact on my life.

LESSONS

1. Your bills are your responsibility, not your lawyer's

When a bill is due, no matter how much you disagree with the amount, pay at least the amount you agree you owe. It is important to show good faith and pay something. Courts consider a case differently if someone is disputing part of a bill than if they are trying to get out of paying anything at all. From the court's perspective, you'll have taken responsibility for at least the undisputed portion of your bill. I'm certainly not saying that you should not challenge an erroneous bill but think carefully and plan wisely. You will be the one in collections, not your lawyer. Because my lawyer advised me not to pay the trucking company, I did not do so; that was a miscalculation on my part.

2. Your court documents are your responsibility, not your lawyer's

As a small business owner, always review your legal briefs. If you don't understand what they say, have your attorney explain the key components and arguments. Remember, lawyers provide a service, and their legal skills are only tools. They are not business owners, and they do not have all the background information about your business. Therefore, you must review their key arguments in any legal brief. I have discovered I frequently need to make corrections, not because my lawyers are inadequate, but because they do not have all the crucial facts about my business operations. Business owners must review all legal documents before submitting them to the court.

3. Think hard before filing that lawsuit

If you're considering filing a lawsuit, review the amount of the dispute versus the potential legal fees. Never enter a lawsuit expecting to gain money, except perhaps in a personal injury case. Contract law is challenging. Often, the only ones who win are the lawyers.

At its core, my dispute with the trucking company concerned less than $3,000. Including the appeal, I spent close to $65,000 on legal fees. With the $134,000 the opposing party claimed I owed plus my $65,000, this dispute, after all was said and done, cost close to $200,000 in legal fees. Paying the initial $2,900 would have been much cheaper, not to mention saving the time, resources, and emotional distress to all parties involved. As a small business owner, exhibit self-control until anger and frustration fades. Don't lose control of your emotions or become manipulated by others who might profit from a lawsuit. Ask yourself these questions: Is it worth my time? Is it worth my emotional energy? Whenever you pursue a lawsuit, your emotions will be drained and you will be less able to attend to anything else in your life.

4. Read anything you sign

I understand how miniscule and long the print may be on a contract, but you must read and be sure you comprehend it. Find a lawyer you can trust who will explain it to you before you sign.

5. Bankruptcy is not your only option

Your business is worth fighting for. When I lost the case in November 2015 and was told I owed the trucking company $72,000, my then-attorney told me to file for bankruptcy. I disagreed, and this became the primary reason I separated from my first counsel.

6. Let God be your counsel

God is my ultimate counsel: that is the foundation for all I do. I regularly read the book of Proverbs, which is full of wisdom regarding how to deal with people, business relationships, and difficult life circumstances. It conveys the wisdom of God's word, which I then confirm with my personal legal research. I have made it a priority to approach legal decisions in this way. Before you consult with others, read the Bible first for direction, whether or not you are a follower of Christ. The wisdom in its pages applies to every human being. I no longer go to legal counsel first, pay thousands of dollars, and then look to the Bible: My priorities have changed, and I suggest yours do as well.

19

NEW BEGINNING, OLD ADVERSARY

As I left the court case behind me, I anticipated a new season. It was 2017, and I started making plans for my business again. Honestly, if I had not won the appellate case, I would have had no idea about my company's future. With such a large amount of money involved, the court could have put a lien on my company's bank accounts, seizing any revenue plus interest. I didn't want to go through that, and I briefly considered closing the business. However, had I closed my business I would have had extreme difficulty pursuing other career options. This is what I love to do and where I excel.

Furthermore, closing the business wouldn't have solved anything. Based on the judgment and the way my company was incorporated, if I closed the business and tried to start another, the trucking company could have then pursued that new company and whatever revenue it made. It was too risky, and closing the business seemed like a dead end.

Thankfully, I won the case and never had to face that issue. My victory led to a new state of mind: "Now there's closure! Now there's time for celebration!" In January 2017, I repainted my office a lively blue color, purchased new furniture, decluttered, and reorganized. It felt like purging and lifting years of burden off of my shoulders.

Shortly after the office facelift, my friend, a faculty member from my alma mater, Biola University, contacted me. Biola was seeking alumni to teach new business classes with an emphasis on international business. My first reaction was, "Wow, that is great! It has been one of my dreams to pass on all the lessons God has taught me in owning my own business."

In mid-spring, I met with the dean of the business school. As we talked, it became apparent that what they were searching for, a part-time adjunct position, would require a lot of time and energy, something I did not have. Rebuilding my company after the devastating lawsuits was already a full-time job and my top priority. Not dissuaded, the dean introduced me to the faculty member in charge of a program mentoring MBA students. After listening to the program's objectives, I decided that it fit my time and experience much better and eagerly agreed to come on board. After an extensive application process, I received clearance during the summer of 2017 to become a Biola business school mentor.

I felt on top of the world and was elated to fulfill my dream of teaching. I was assigned an MBA mentee to meet with at least once a month. I thoroughly enjoyed sharing what I had learned to prepare my mentee for a future in business. It seemed like everything was going my way.

My responsibilities started to increase as I accepted other opportunities at the business school. In addition to what I originally agreed to do, I eventually served as a panelist for presentations by graduating seniors, a team coach in the school's student start-up competition, a reviewer for student business plans and concept papers, and a presenter for various classes of special topics in my field.

From the day I met with the dean until Thanksgiving, about three months in total, I traveled to the campus every other week for some event of another. All told, I was spending nearly half of my time there while holding down my full-time job. Needless to say, I was exhausted but found the experience extremely rewarding.

One event in which I participated became a significant turning point for me. I was asked to speak at a "fireside chat," an informal gathering for business students. I spoke for an hour and a half to a number of students about my career and being an entrepreneur. The goal was to encourage students who were considering starting their own businesses and to help them integrate their faith into their business practices. This informal gathering became the very first forum I had in which to share many of the stories in this book.

I remember that evening clearly; in publicly retelling these stories for the first time, I became emotional. Right then, in front of all those students, I saw with light bulb clarity that I had never allowed myself to emotionally process all that I had gone through over the last few years. Even though it had been a year since the last lawsuit, I was still raw with anger and hurt, and it showed. I barely held it together.

It wasn't exactly the way I had planned to share my stories with the students, but nevertheless, God made use of me. After my talk, several students introduced themselves to me, and I kept in touch with them through the end of the semester. They seemed genuinely touched, because I was willing to be open, honest, and vulnerable.

That night should have felt like a triumph. For the first time, I shared my trials and my failures, my victories, and my deliverance through God.

But it didn't feel that way at all. In fact, I remember feeling just the opposite: my spirit was oppressed. I was emotionally drained and physically exhausted, and yet I could not sleep.

Because something else happened that night.

20

"YOU HAVE CANCER"

As the evening of my fireside chat with the Biola business students came to a close, a man who was clearly not a student appeared at the back of the crowd and joined the Q&A. I soon realized that he was not friendly: he inquired about my lawsuits, implying that I had caused the problems. His queries felt like an attack, and my body reacted. I felt like I had been stabbed in the heart; it was as if a dark force was using this man to stir up a spiritual disturbance within me. That night, I tossed and turned, and the next morning I woke up with aches and pains all over my body. This continued, and four days later, on Thanksgiving, I was so sick I could not get out of bed.

My whole body had given out, and I was not even strong enough to drive myself to the emergency room. I didn't want to call 911, as my problem didn't seem life-threatening, but something was wrong with me. Then, the day after Thanksgiving, I discovered a four-inch lump in my chest. I had never felt it before, and it seemed as if it had appeared in less than 24 hours. When I pressed on the lump, it was as hard as a rock, but it wasn't painful; I didn't feel a sense of urgency about it or the need to visit the emergency room. Instead, I waited to see if it would go away by itself. I normally use Chinese medicine for self-treatment before I see a doctor or make use of Western medicine. But after a week of this without any improvement, I finally made an appointment to see my doctor. She was shocked when she saw the size of the lump: right away she told me, "You have cancer."

21

THE MYSTERY DEEPENS

My doctor told me to go see an oncologist and referred me to her husband. She then took some samples, because there was some liquid seeping out of the lump. However, the results were inconclusive. As a result, my doctor told me I needed the tests any other cancer patient would have, including a mammogram and a biopsy to obtain tissue samples.

She and her husband, the oncologist, were both sure I had cancer. But I knew, deep in my heart, that this lump was not cancer. It had appeared overnight and was rock-hard, which is inconsistent with cancer. Yet, I followed their advice and had more tests done at the local hospital. Meanwhile, the lump continued to grow larger and, unlike when it first appeared, it became painful.

My doctors decided that I needed exploratory surgery to determine what the lump was and if it could be drained. My family doctor recommended a good friend, a physician working at a nationally recognized hospital who specialized in cancers of the chest. Since it was so close to Christmas, many physicians were not accepting patients. Thankfully, this doctor made time to see me. His initial response was, "Wow, that is not normal." Just two days before Christmas, he operated on me after-hours and tried to drain whatever was inside the lump. He suspected that inflammation had created the lump and was causing my pain, which seemed to be a reasonable diagnosis.

My first biopsy indicated that there was no cancer, but based on the doctor's observations and to err on the side of caution, he performed a second biopsy two weeks later. He ruptured my skin using a long needle inserted well below the surface to get multiple tissue samples. The process was very painful, but the doctor assured me it would enable him to make sure I didn't have cancer. The second biopsy confirmed that it was not cancer, but the lump wasn't going away. The surgeon then prescribed some very strong antibiotics, but none worked to destroy or dissolve the lump.

Finally, the doctor determined that the lump was related to tuberculosis, since the lump was fairly close to my lungs. I had major surgery on January 8, 2018; the surgeon opened me up for a third time and used scissors to cut away the tissues causing the lump and hardness. He also took additional samples to test for TB. However, all the results came back negative: no TB.

By this time, I suffered from a huge amount of pain. When I entered recovery after my third surgery, I told the nurse that I could not function due to pain. She told me that I was already on the maximum dose of painkillers, but I needed more, preferably morphine. God bless her, she somehow found a way to increase my dosage.

After surgery, I had appointments every week so the doctor could check the wound and see whether the lump was shrinking. I told the doctor, "You removed or ruled out everything you suspected was causing the lump, but it's still there." My doctor responded, "It looks better now;

it looks good." The doctor told my mother and good friend, who has a medical background, that he had removed everything and that I would be fine.

But I knew I wasn't better. My condition worsened: the area of incision became badly infected.

22

OUT OF OPTIONS

I was out of options and had no idea what to do next. The doctor wanted to do yet another surgery to take out the lump: surgery was the only treatment he knew. But I put my foot down and refused. I already had an infection! More surgery was not an option. It would be too dangerous for my body, and so I made a deliberate choice for my own health.

My infection could have been avoided if I had properly cared for the wound after surgery. Somehow, I did not receive instructions about post-surgical care. By the grace of God, one of the women in my Wednesday Bible study fellowship was a doctor at the same hospital as my surgeon. She instructed me on wound care, something my surgeon failed to do. But although I immediately followed her advice, the infection did not subside but continued to worsen.

My doctors knew I was frustrated, but although they had ruled out cancer and TB, the lump remained and they did not have an answer. They next wondered if the problem could be related to a virus. My surgeon referred me to the hospital's main campus, which had a large virology department. My appointment with the virology specialist was near the end of January. I had twenty different lab tests in one day. Yes, 20! Amazingly, the results came back within hours: there was no sign of cancer, a virus, or any other unusual disease.

In February, I returned to the virology department a few more times. I told the doctor that two weeks before I got sick I had competed in a mud run. I figured this additional information might be useful in determining a cause for my infection. As a result, the doctors requested tests for fungi, allergies, staph infections, and other dirt-based issues. Guess what? The results again came back negative. In fact, ironically the lab work showed that I was in very good health.

This was occurring right as I became involved in Biola's mentorship program and was establishing a rhythm of activities at the university. But because of my illness I had to cancel all activities during the spring semester.

This became an immensely challenging season. Unexplained physical issues are demoralizing, confusing, and painful. My doctors were the best of the best, and yet nobody seemed able to treat me, and nobody could give me an explanation. Finally, after all the viral tests came back negative, my doctors order yet another surgery. I walked out of the hospital. I'd had it!

Instead, I went to see a Chinese doctor who had successfully treated me ten years earlier for a skin-related disease after all other treatments had failed. She diagnosed me with malnutrition and a lack of a certain protein in my body. My cure-all? Eat more meat. She prescribed Chinese herbal medicine to drain my lump, but it did not work. And while I began a high-protein diet, there was no change. Nobody could figure out the mystery. Where else could I turn? It was only when I reached bottom that I thought: "I wonder what God has to say about this."

23

THE ANSWER

My health crisis dragged on for months. By April, I felt God nudging me to see my family doctor again. I had not seen her since the first week of December, and when she saw me she was shocked. All three incision sites were badly infected, and blood seeping out of each incision. It was rank. I pleaded with her: "I need your recommendation. These other doctors did many, many things, but they couldn't help me. The lump is still there. And now it's worse, because I have an infection, the incisions have not healed, and I am still bleeding."

Her first course of action: focus on the wound. For an entire hour, she cleaned and sterilized my wounds. She did not give me any medication, only large doses of high-grade supplements to boost my immune system. This included a bottle of high-dosage curcumin, the main constituent of turmeric powder. Curcumin has long been used in traditional medicine to treat inflammation, and she prescribed two per day. My appointment was Friday April 27, and when I awoke on April 28, the lump had disappeared. It was like a balloon had deflated. The lump was there, and then it wasn't. The only things that had changed were that my wound had been cleaned and I had taken a high dosage of high-quality curcumin. I did not go back to the hospital: I did not need to. I stopped all the antibiotics and focused on taking the high-quality supplements. My only remaining concern was the incisions on my chest. Though they were relatively small, to me they looked huge. More importantly, blood still occasionally seeped through the incisions.

In July, I took a trip to Hong Kong and visited a friend who is a cancer survivor. She introduced me to a treatment called Origin Point Therapy (OPT). In Asian countries, OPT has been used to treat all manner of ailments and illnesses, from diabetes to terminal cancer. My friend went through OPT and it worked so well for her that she went through three years of training to be able to treat others.

OPT is similar to acupuncture. It assumes that the root cause of disease is typically elsewhere in the body (the "origin point"), and that treatment should thus address this underlying cause rather than the symptoms. There are origin points along the spine and at seven other points in the body: the head, shoulder, elbow, hand, hip, ankle, and instep.

I went to a clinic my friend recommended. My therapist told me that even though the lump was on my chest, the origin point was located on my back. Obviously, nobody at the hospital had ever considered that possibility. The therapist massaged me in a very specific way on the point that triggered the inflammation. After the massage, she gave me hot compresses for my back and ginger tea to drink. By the next morning, the wounds had stopped bleeding, and I have not had any seepage since. By the fall of 2018, my health was the best it had ever been. God had given me a second chance.

LESSONS

1. Listen to the Great Physician

Throughout these lessons I have stressed how important it is to listen to God. If I had not listened to God when He said to return to my family doctor and pay attention to what she recommended, I don't think I would have gotten results so quickly, or maybe at all.

2. Health is a priority

If you don't take care of your health, it will affect other aspects of your life: your business, spiritual walk, relationships, and even finances.

I will admit that I wasn't eating a balanced diet. Protein is very important for the body, and I wasn't consuming enough. In addition, I was not taking supplements. As we get older, our bodies are unable to absorb nutrients as well as when we're younger. Our bodies need help through high-dose, high-grade supplements to give our bodies the vitamins and minerals we need. I am now completely committed to taking my supplements every day, no matter how busy I am.

I also take care of myself in other ways. I meditate, which is like a daily quiet time. Almost every day I use the infrared sauna at my gym for detoxification. I've added daily hydro-massage to my routine. As a result, I feel healthier and have more energy. My immune system has become stronger, and when I'm around people who are sick, I am less susceptible to infection.

3. Poor health is costly

My hospital and medical bills totaled $50,000 before insurance. Even after the insurance payout, my out-of-pocket expenses came to almost $6,000. Receiving medical treatment is much more expensive in America than preventative measures such as taking good supplements every day. Even the best supplements, which may cost around $80 for a two-month supply (less than $1.50 per day), are far cheaper than getting sick and needing high-cost treatments such as surgery.

4. Your health is your responsibility, not your doctor's

When the doctor told me I had cancer, I was not scared; I believed wholeheartedly that it wasn't true. When she insisted I see an oncologist, I rejected her advice and persistently requested additional tests. When it comes to your health, take control and make your own decisions. You must be your own advocate: no one else will do it for you. Don't let doctors make the decisions; they don't know your body the way you do. They treat you based on what they see and hear from you.

A good doctor is an important aid to your health, but only that: an aid. They are not God, they are not perfect, and they do not have the final decision. You do. Listen to your body, especially when it comes to surgery, because surgery may result in unexpected side effects. Conduct research and get a second and third opinion. Don't treat any surgery as routine. Search for alternatives before treating your illness through aggressive surgery. Even though my surgeon was a doctor at a nationally recognized hospital and did a good job of minimizing my wounds, something went wrong. He failed to give me instructions on post-surgical care, which resulted in my wounds getting infected.

Pay attention to your body and live a balanced life. You need to be intentional and make self-care a priority in order to be efficient and effective in everything you do.

5. Pay regular attention to your physical health

Eating a balanced diet is important. Even with the best supplements, the food you eat and how you eat it are very important. For example, I used to not eat anything all day and then a big meal for dinner. This is unhealthy for multiple reasons, the least of which is that your blood sugar can go through the roof, which can be very dangerous. If you can, always choose healthy meals with fresh ingredients and eat three or four meals a day.

6. Pay regular attention to your mental health

God created us with a body that can heal itself if we provide it with the right mix of natural ingredients to counteract anything unhealthy going on inside us. Our bodies, minds, and souls are very closely connected. In my situation, I had inflammation because my life was out of alignment. I truly believe that it related to the stress from the trials I went through. It all accumulated while I wasn't paying attention.

Even if you do everything else right, failing to pay attention to stress will cost you both physical and mental health. Your mind, soul, and body are not separate systems: they were designed to work as one. Life is challenging, and when your body is not operating at an optimal level (or even at a normal level), it will affect your business, relationships, self-image, finances, sleep, everything. Be intentional and make it a habit to check your stress levels. Find something to relieve stress on a regular basis, such as exercise, meditation, personal retreats, or counseling.

24

BUT THAT'S MY NAME!

In May 2015, all the phones in the office began ringing off the hook. Normally during this time of the year, busy phone traffic indicates one thing: delivery problems. Yet all my books were on schedule and there was no sign of any unplanned issues, such as the yearbook debacle that had taken place two years earlier.

I thought I was about to enter a peaceful season. The case between my East Coast client and myself had just completed, and the IRS investigation had closed. My company had received an apology from the IRS earlier that year, and I thought that would be the end of our litigation. I also assumed at the time that the trucking case had been resolved; the lower court had just awarded the $2,900 judgment against me and my company. I thought we were free and clear of any more legal issues, and I was ready to relax and celebrate. I even took a restful, lengthy vacation to Thailand with my family. "All the legal fiascos are finally all over," I thought. But I relaxed too soon: May 2015 brought with it yet another extraordinary business problem.

The calls that flooded our lines were strange: students and parents requesting yearbooks. My company has never taken direct orders for yearbooks; we only produce the books. Individual schools handle the actual ordering and purchasing.

I decided to answer one call myself to better understand the situation. It was with a parent whose daughter attended a school I had never heard of, somewhere in Arizona that was not one of my clients. I was as confused as the parent.

"Ma'am, are you sure you have the right company? This is United Yearbook."

"Yes," she said. "You came out to the school to take her senior picture. I misplaced the postcard you gave her with your Phoenix address, so I was hoping to just call you to order the yearbook. United Yearbook, right?"

My head started to spin. We don't take student pictures, and we don't have a Phoenix address. Could there be another United Yearbook?

At first, I had thought the incoming phone calls meant new business: new schools looking for a publisher for next year's yearbook publications. How wonderful that would've been. But, like the mother I talked to, the people on the other end were mainly parents wanting to order a single yearbook. These calls became more frequent, tying up all our lines. Soon, we were getting twenty phone calls an hour, all day long, even on Saturday. I did some investigating and found that most of the callers found our phone number online. I then discovered that, although they were parents and students at several different schools, they were all from Arizona. When we asked them how they found our website, every last one of them said, "I just googled your company name, because your company's other website didn't have a phone number." Our other website? What was going on?

It didn't take long for my staff to find a company in Arizona publishing yearbooks under the name United Yearbooks. United Yearbooks of Arizona was a subcontractor for a larger parent company, also in Arizona, called United Images. As best as I could determine, the only business United Images conducted prior to 2015 was as a photography company. In 2015, they branched out into the yearbook publishing industry, calling their new yearbook company United Yearbooks. The problem was that United Yearbook already existed: it was me!

25

MAKING MY NAME MINE

A few months before the deluge of phone calls began, in the fall of 2015, I attended the Conference of California Bar Associations (CCBA), a four-day convention where lawyers, paralegals, and law students attend workshops and panels. I had attended this conference for several years, each time meeting prominent lawyers while obtaining free legal advice from experts and panel events. Most speakers were lawyers or justices from different courts of law. I found the event extremely beneficial and enlightening in my line of work.

The main purpose of the convention is to teach attendees new materials and review old ones from law school. I attended workshops on copyright and how to file appeals. The information couldn't have come at a better time, as I soon came face to face with a new fight: this one regarding trademark infringement.

The week after the phone calls began, I called the main office of United Images. I introduced myself as the owner of United Yearbook and told them that I'd like to speak to either their owner or their lawyer. The person with whom I spoke did not sound surprised to hear from me but promised to pass on my name and phone number. However, I never received a response, and the company continued to use my business's name. I faced a dilemma.

Using the knowledge I had gained from the CCBA on how to investigate potential trademark and copyright infringement and how to protect myself when my mark is compromised or infringed, I went to work. I realized that although I had been using the same United Yearbook wordmark and company logo since 2008, I had not officially registered them as trademarks, a necessary process to enforce my rights. Being the first company to use that name and logo gave me some protection. However, if I wanted to sue someone for using my name and logo, I would need to have them already registered with the U.S. Patent and Trademark Office. I gathered evidence indicating that I had been using the United Yearbook name since 2008: trade brochures and advertisements, invoices and contracts, my website, even the yearbooks themselves. With these prepared, I immediately filed an application for trademark. At the same time, however, I learned that United Images had also filed the name United Yearbooks with the U.S. Patent and Trademark Office a few days after I first contacted them. How cheeky and underhanded of them, to try to subvert my efforts by beating me to the punch.

This situation required specific measures. First, I needed to publicly publish a notice of trademark, so others would know I was about to register this name. Second, once United Images published their notice of trademark, I had to immediately file a dispute notice.

This was how the legal proceeding started. I was armed with legal evidence and, upon receiving my documentation, the court had to see evidence on whether using an already-existing name would confuse people. For example, Apple Inc. and AppleOne have similar names, but AppleOne is an employment agency and Apple Inc. is a multinational technology company: there isn't much chance that people will get the two confused. But two almost identical companies—United Yearbook and United Yearbooks—within the same publishing industry is a completely different story.

I already had evidence that people were confused: records of phone calls from parents who had gone to our website and called our number, thinking they were contacting this other company. When people looked for the other company on Google or social media, my website came up. I was not about to allow this new company to piggyback on the millions of dollars I spent on advertising and the thousands of hours I spent building goodwill with clients. In addition, not only was this new company using the United Yearbooks name to profit off my brand, they also sold my name to others. They were franchising a brand they had no rights to, one that included such companies as United Yearbooks Arizona/Phoenix, United Yearbooks Arizona/Prescott, and so forth. I couldn't believe what they were up to.

I started interviewing lawyers who specialized in trademark cases. With the lessons I learned from my previous legal battles still fresh in my mind, I retained a law firm that did not charge me a large retainer upfront. Instead, I hired a California firm with reasonable rates, that was local, and that seemed to have a solid track record of the type of work I needed. My lawyer sent a cease and desist letter to United Images that essentially stated: "Stop what you're doing. If you don't, then we will sue you." As expected, this did not stop United Images. They insisted, with no solid evidence, that they were the first to use the United Yearbooks name.

I had no choice but to aggressively continue with the legal proceedings. I could have compromised and agreed to let United Images use
the name United Yearbooks only in Arizona, but I decided this was not
an option. I already had clients in Arizona, and I didn't want to confuse
them: what if they thought we were the same company? Additionally,
I wanted the endless phone calls to stop. Or what if someone googled
"United Yearbook" and their company came up first? How could I be sure
they would only take in-state clients? Could I trust them to abide by any
agreement or did I need a court order for them to take me seriously?

The only answer to these questions was to proceed legally. There
could be only one United Yearbook: me. That meant I had to become involved in additional legal dealings. With my mind firmly made up, I dove
back into the legal world to ensure this problem would never happen
again.

26

TRADEMARKS ARE...TRICKY

Thus began another legal battle. I started the proceedings against United Images in late 2015 and it consumed the entirety of 2016. Filing after filing of court documents, as well as months of delays and extended procedures became my nightmare. United Images changed their legal representation multiple times, which I saw as a positive sign. If a party in a legal case frequently changes lawyers, it often means that the lawyers do not believe in the case. Even my own lawyers told me that it might mean the previous law firms had dropped them or they were not paying their legal bills.

In 2017, we finally came to the discovery stage of the suit, or the part of the process where each party brings out their evidence. I had mountains of evidence to show I had been using the name for several years: thankfully, my previous experiences had given me the know-how to compile everything that was needed. I submitted nearly a hundred documents bearing the United Yearbook name: invoices, contracts, and brochures. Meanwhile, United Images had absolutely nothing to prove that they had used the name before I did or prior to 2015.

A few weeks later, United Images dropped their attempt to register the name. This was a huge victory: once they dropped out, my registration of the United Yearbook wordmark became official with the U.S. Patent and Trademark Office. Shortly thereafter, the logo was also officially registered. I filed a similar registration in Canada, just to cover my bases. Everything seemed settled in my favor. However, it turned out that things weren't so simple, although I now had a legal leg to stand on.

My lawyer asked me what came next. I didn't know: I thought we were done. He then told me that as the official owner, I had to protect my trademark. That meant I had the right to sue if another company in the same industry used even a key part of my registered name. If United Images attempted to publish yearbooks under their parent name, he continued, I could sue them for using the word "United." In fact, he said, I should sue them.

Trademark law is tricky. Getting a trademark is only the beginning; then you must protect the trademark. If I discovered United Images was publishing yearbooks under any name that included the word "United" and I did nothing about it, I could lose my trademark. If I ever decided their company was a serious threat to my business and I wanted to pursue legal action, the court could say, "Sorry, Sarah. By failing to act at the time of trademark issuance, you granted United Images a waiver. You knowingly let them use the name all this time, so we're assuming you didn't care before. If you didn't care before, you can't expect us to make them change it now." Tricky!

I wanted to clean house and not leave any loophole that could come back to bite me. My legal counsel explained that in order to protect my trademark, I had to force United Images to give up the word "United" completely or force them out of the yearbook business. This decision had extensive consequences for both parties, and it made me uncomfortable. At the same time, I looked into my finances. My law firm's fees were within reason, but I had spent a sizable chunk of money, tens of thousands of dollars. I have yet to summarize how much I spent on this lawsuit in total, but I know it was an immense amount between 2015 and 2018.

Meanwhile, United Images was still using the name United Yearbooks. To protect the name I had just trademarked, I needed to demand that they stop. I told my lawyer, "I know I have the right, but I don't want more litigation." Instead, I requested he send them a letter, another cease and desist, telling them to stop using the name United Yearbooks. Now that I was the legal, registered owner of that trademark, I thought a cease and desist letter might carry more weight. And it might have, if my lawyer had done what I asked him to do.

Instead, he sent a very aggressive email without my consent. I specifically instructed him to notify me before sending the letter. I wanted to see it first so I could approve the language and wording; the last thing I wanted was to trigger an escalation or another lawsuit. But my lawyer went against my wishes. Here is an excerpt from his email:

> "As you may know, our client asserts superior rights to all UNITED formative trademarks, including UNITED IMAGES. For the foregoing reasons, we demand that your client United Images Holdings, LLC immediately cease and desist from any further use of any UNITED formative trademarks."

The email went out, and things escalated fast. Imagine my surprise in March 2018 when someone delivered a legal summons to my office. The tables had turned: United Images was now coming after me.

27

COUNTERPUNCHES, CONVICTION, AND COMPROMISE

The delivery was a request for a declaratory judgment, something common in trademark or patent cases. One side sends a cease and desist, then the other party files for a declaratory judgment. It is usually an attempt by the infringer to force the other party to act, as if to say, "Stop threatening me. Either put up or shut up." If granted by the court, a declaratory judgment forces the trademark owner to decide whether or not they want to sue. Filing for a declaratory judgment was a smart move on the part of United Images: they beat me to the punch, and I now had to defend my trademark in an Arizona courtroom.

It took me a while to determine what United Images wanted, because I still hadn't seen the threatening email from my lawyers. Everything soon became clear, however: United Images was asking the Arizona judge to allow them to use the word "United" in their name for perpetuity. My law firm had sent the threatening letter telling them to stop using the word "United" altogether while they were trying to legally register their company name, United Images, as a trademark.

United Images retained one of the biggest law firms in Washington D.C., specialists in trademark law, to challenge our wordmark on United Yearbook. They filed two petitions with the U.S. Patent and Trademark

Office to cancel my United Yearbook marks registered in January and one requesting them to reverse my registration of the logo and wordmark.

My trademark lawyer told me I had the legal right to protect my trademark and sue United Images, forcing them to either give up the word "United" or leave the yearbook industry. I held the legal right to the name, as shown by my registered trademark. United Images, however, chose to force the issue and try to have my trademark disallowed. If they succeeded, I would be unable to force them to stop using the word "United."

A calculated legal strategy on their part, they tried to use this declaratory judgment filing to put me on the defensive and make it more difficult to go after them for using "United" in their company name. I had wondered earlier if they had enough money for a legal defense, and now they were likely wondering if I had enough money to fight on two fronts at the same time. This was a preemptive strike and got my attention. We were in a sparring match: who would blink and give in first? Was this small Arizona company represented by a large, expensive international firm, or had they paid the firm a smaller amount just to send a couple of threatening letters? Anybody could file a petition; I knew I had the evidence to win.

But it takes money to fight a lawsuit. After spending the last few years frantically rebuilding my business, I again liquidated more of my dwindling assets. I had come this far. If I didn't defend my logo and wordmark, then what was the point of spending all the money to defend my company? I felt that I had no choice. I prayed about it, and God gave me complete peace. More money had drained away, but I felt like my future was safe.

I wasn't happy with my law firm, however. Disappointed and frustrated, I felt like their impetuousness and failure to follow my instructions had brought about this new round of problems. I had a lot invested in them, though, and trying to bring a new firm up to speed at this point seemed unwise. I decided to keep their retainer, but I now monitored everything they did. I read every brief and made sure they brought me up to date on every item and correspondence. By now it was late spring 2018, and I was in the middle of another busy yearbook season. Despite my hectic schedule, I followed through on all the legal matters without excuse, reading every legal brief and item of paperwork filed. I made sure the lead attorney copied me on everything.

I eventually figured out what United Images really wanted from me. They were willing to stop using the name "United Yearbooks"; they just wanted to be able use "United" in their name. That's all. That's all they had wanted from the beginning. It was only after reading my lawyer's aggressive letter that they decided to respond in kind. Looking back on it now, if we had put aside our egos, we might have been able to talk civilly without the lawyers and legal fees.

It felt like we were trapped in a cycle benefitting only the lawyers, and I wanted it all to end. I had responded to their aggressiveness in kind, which my lawyer had caused in the first place. In May 2018, I gave my lawyers specific instructions: this matter needed a compromise and to come to a mutually satisfactory agreement. This time, I wanted to do it my way.

We eventually drew up a settlement that brought everything to a close. My lawyers worked with United Images' lawyers to draft an acceptable compromise and to devise a settlement agreement that both parties signed. Subsequently, United Images withdrew the declaratory judgment request and petitions with the U.S. Patent and Trademark Office. Hallelujah! United Yearbook, my company, would maintain its logo and wordmark as exclusive intellectual property with the U.S. Patent and Trademark Office. We agreed that United Images could continue to use "United" in their wordmark. I was satisfied, because the deal seemed fair. I was also relieved: as of July 16, 2018, this whole nightmare was over.

It had been seven long years, almost to the exact date, since my troubles began. I sat alone in my office, in the company I had fought so hard to protect, thinking, "This case is over, but something else, some other crisis, must be looming around the corner." This had been the pattern over the past seven years, after all. I was tired, physically and emotionally spent in every way. This moment was the closest I had come to financial ruin. The stack of invoices coming in from lawyers was much higher than that sent to customers. I had been fighting, and fighting, and fighting, and for what?

I suddenly had a picture in my head of a young teenage boy named David trying to fight the giant Goliath in King Saul's oversized armor. Then, I heard a still, small voice: "Sarah?"

I was at rock bottom, at the end of my strength. "Can it be done?" I cried out into the empty room. "God, can it just be over? No more?"

It can be hard to hear a voice that doesn't make any sound. But I heard it. I heard it in the heart of my soul.

"Are *you* done, Sarah?" His voice said gently.

I put my head down on the desk. "Yes," I whispered, "I'm done."

"Then it's done," He answered.

LESSONS

1. The final decisions are yours, not your lawyer's

Don't make the same mistake I did and allow your lawyer to make the final call. Whether I moved ahead with litigation should've been my decision and mine only.

2. Your communications are your responsibility, not your lawyer's

Make it a priority to review everything your attorney sends to the opposing party before it becomes official. Sometimes the words lawyers use can sound threatening. Lawyers excel in this arena because it helps their case, even though that may not have been your intention.

3. Pay attention to the tone of your legal communication

Make sure the tone of all written communication is what you want it to be. You don't want your lawyer to misrepresent you or give a false impression of how you want to handle the case. Certain words and phrases can trigger emotions. This may cause the other party to respond more aggressively and in turn cost you more money.

4. Register your trademarks

When you invest in your company name and brand, you must file an application with the U.S. Patent and Trademark Office. Don't leave your mark unprotected. The only way you retain the right to sue if someone starts using your logo or company name in the same industry is to have an official registration with the Trademark Office. The filing is inexpensive and easy to do: anyone who can read instructions can complete the form. It cost me less than $300 to file my trademark. Of course there are also law firms that can help you file; their fees should not be that costly.

5. Don't be scared of a big law firm

More often than not, a small company will hire a larger law firm just for tactical show. Be strong: The truth will always prevail. Facts, hard evidence, and the correct legal strategy will be on your side and help you win.

6. Clean house

When you are in a legal battle, "clean house" so that you do not leave any loophole that may trigger a potential return of the same issue. Completely address and resolve all issues involving your case, even though it may cost you an extra thousand dollars in legal fees to accomplish this. For example, United Images wanted my permission to let them use the name United Yearbooks in Arizona. I stood my ground, retaining the exclusive rights to my company's name regardless of territories to avoid confusion. It's worth it in the long run. If you leave certain issues undone, it is only a matter of time before they resurface. Then you will regret that you had not taken care of it before.

7. It's not about you: it never was

The biggest lesson I learned, not just in this particular trial but in all the trials described in this book, is that everything doesn't happen because of you or for your sake.

28

THE WORD IS GRATITUDE

As I wrote this book, I wondered how to bring it to a close. How do I put a capstone on all the lessons I have learned? Was there an apex, an ultimate theme? And how did these events change me? If I had to pick one final word, what would it be? I prayed about it, and I heard nothing for a couple of days. I waited. Then, in His time, God answered me. He said, "I'm going to give you the word." But then He kept silent again for another week. At last, the word came to me: *gratitude*.

The word came rushing like a flood into my head. I'm overwhelmed with gratitude for my seven years of non-stop tribulation. How is that possible? How could someone be overwhelmed with gratitude when they have gone through hell? My friends and my family—especially my mother—saw me through these seven years, and even they wondered how I could come out of it and be grateful. How can tribulation and gratitude coincide?

I believe God wants me to say, in closing, that it's because of Him I was able to get through it all. It's not about me: it's about Him!

Coming through the storms revealed that God was strengthening and working in me throughout the entire process.

In all the stories in this book, I was dealing with two or three challenges simultaneously. There was no respite, no break, no time to regroup. It was one thing after another, many times at the same time. But when the last legal situation ended in July 2018, everything stopped. There were no more letters or threats, no more harassing phone calls, no more allegations of suspicious activity. As of today, in April 2019, things have remained calm. I am simply in awe. I must admit that for a few months I could not appreciate the silence or the lack of trials. I was suspicious and nervous, waiting for another trial. I knew something bad must be lurking around the corner.

Yet again, in that still, small voice, God made it clear to me: "No, this is it. All your tribulations have come to an end." Will I have challenges ahead of me? Of course. The most significant impact of these last seven years is that they changed my perspective on trials: how I view and respond to them. Before these trials, my response was, "Great. Another tribulation. I knew it!" Now I look at them as opportunities for God to tell His stories and to fulfill His purposes.

On the career front, it feels like I have been given a brand-new business. October is usually a slow season for the yearbook and printing industry, but last October I got referrals from both old and new customers and clients coming out of nowhere. It was as if God was saying to me, "I still have a plan for your business—for *our* business. The pain I allowed you to go through for these seven years will not be wasted—I am doing something new, and you are going to use the wisdom you gleaned during those seven years and apply it in this new season. I'm opening doors for you."

I am more relaxed now: when things do happen unexpectedly (and they still do), I don't panic or get anxious. I have learned to embrace the moment and the lessons in each experience, knowing that I will learn something new about God through every last one. I also learned new things about myself and how to grow into the excellent businesswoman I aspire to be. My new approach to difficulties is impacting the people around me in a positive way.

Moving forward, I am determined to handle new trials differently; the solutions are not about me. It's not about me figuring out how to handle attacks and oppression or deal with all the crazy stuff that happens. Instead, I view these events as opportunities for God to show up and make His name known, so I can encourage people to tell more stories about Him.

It's not about me. It never was.

29

NOT THE END

I'm just a normal person. I boarded a plane from Hong Kong to the United States as a naive 18-year-old with a British accent. I had just two pieces of luggage and a teddy bear under my arm. From that tender beginning to where I am today, God has written all my stories for the past thirty years. This year, as I turn 48, I want to share these stories with you. Looking back, it doesn't feel like thirty years. Yet it is obvious how God helped me become the person I am today.

I understand that my stories might intimidate you and that you may think, "Oh, the terrible things that could happen in the business world! You just can't trust people!" But that is not the purpose of this book. Instead, it is to express how God, in the midst of my trials, led me to grow and opened doors for me. He put people in my path to help me get through these circumstances, such as the retired presiding judge assigned to my case and who eventually found in my favor. There were many such individuals who assisted me along the way.

There will be storms and troubles in the future. But before my recent trials, I would have considered anything unexpected as a tribulation. When I finished my last legal case in July 2018, God started working on my perspective. He began teaching me to view unexpected situations differently. I no longer get tripped up, angry, or frustrated. In the past, I would lose my patience, and this would affect the people around me. Now I no longer react in such a way; I know that every time something unexpected happens, God purposely put that challenge in my way to lead me in another direction.

I've started to see a pattern in my experiences. If a desired business relationship did not work out, previously I would have become disappointed. I would question myself, thinking, "Oh, what did I do wrong? What could I have said or done differently?" It truly was all about me, about my ability to fix things, my ability to create opportunities or to make things happen. God was not included in the equation. Now my perspective is different: when something does not go as expected, I stop and pray. I've learned that the process of waiting is important. I have learned to wait until God confirms, with more incidents, that He is leading me in a certain direction and a better path for me.

In the past, I tried to fix things before going to Him. If I expected things to happen by a certain time, and they didn't, I tried to fix them on my own. I made additional phone calls, sent additional emails, or tried to get the other person to respond. I no longer do this: I now restrain myself from trying to fix things or running off ahead of God's timing.

That's the lesson of this final section and the pinnacle of this whole book: be aware of where God is in life's unexpected experiences. Why did He allow this to happen? What is He trying to say to you? What is He leading you toward, and what is He leading you away from? I leave you with two final lessons. First, truly understand that God is part of the equation, even when unexpected things happen. Second, wait, pray, and read God's Word, for He will show you why and what.

I know there may be some reading this book who do not have faith in God, and I want to speak to you directly. You have seen that Christian faith is a big part of my life. I deeply encourage you to think about God and to seriously ask, "Who is this God she's been talking about throughout the book?"

I didn't know God existed until my oldest sister invited me to church when I was eight years old. My understanding increased through grades 6 to 12, when I attended United Christian College, one of the finest Christian schools in Hong Kong. During these years, I learned from the Bible and many of the teachers who invested in me, spiritually nurturing my growing faith. These dedicated teachers became spiritual advisors. Their investment has continued to impact my life, and I continue to keep in touch with them years later. When I began my first semester at Biola University, I chose to dedicate my life to Jesus Christ. That was a defining moment for me, and I truly integrated my faith in daily life. Throughout college, my faith in God continued to develop. After graduation I initially struggled to integrate my faith and my work, but I never quit pursuing Him. God and His Word continue to be my guiding light.

If you don't know God but want to have Him in your life, you don't need to go to a temple like many Chinese do. You don't need to follow rules and regulations or try to be good enough for God. John 3:16 says, "God so loved the world that He gave His one and only Son, that whosoever believes in Him shall not perish but have everlasting life." To trust God is simple, like a child's trust. The first step is to admit that you sin, that you do wrong things and hurt yourself and others. No matter what you do, you cannot make things right with your own efforts. Second, recognize that Jesus Christ is God. He died to forgive you of your sins and rose again from the dead three days later. Only He can make you clean and a new person. Believe Christ is who He says He is and completely surrender yourself to Him. Then the Holy Spirit, who is God, will come into your life and help you understand more about who He is. To continue to grow in your new faith, make it a priority to become involved in a church community that has solid biblical teachings. It's that simple.

I'm overwhelmed with gratitude for the wealth of experiences with which God has entrusted me. As I look back, I believe they were not tribulations or trials, but rather valuable life lessons from above.

I'm grateful for what God has done and is doing in my life. I'm grateful that I have this opportunity to share these stories with you. I pray you are encouraged and that you find these valuable lessons a message of hope. May God bless you.

WHO IS SARAH Y. TSE?

Born in Hong Kong, Sarah Y. Tse contracted tuberculosis at birth and spent the first year of her life in the hospital. Upon discharge, she exhibited signs of autism and learning disabilities. These issues plagued her until she attended a Catholic elementary school and received much-needed help and personal attention from caring nuns and teachers. Out of concern for Sarah, one of her elementary teachers strongly encouraged Sarah's mother to "nurture this child, because she has great potential to succeed." Taking this advice, Sarah progressed academically and in her communication skills.

Sarah's mental and physical toughness came from a strong genetic background. The Tse family is descended from Mongolian warriors, who escaped to South China during the World Wars. Once the Age of Warriors ended, many turned to scholarship, law enforcement, and business pursuits. Sarah's father, who grew up in Hong Kong, found his way into law enforcement and worked for the British government for thirty-five years. He gained years of experience tracking down organized crime leaders, specifically the Triad groups. Sarah's mother made a living as a part-time seamstress while maintaining the household as a full-time homemaker. Though she did not finish high school, she taught herself to invest in foreign currency exchanges. Her wise investing produced profits that enabled the family to pay for their children's college expenses. Sarah received both the wisdom of her mother and her father's sense of justice.

Involved in many extracurricular activities throughout junior and senior high school, Sarah displayed a natural talent in art but was also proficient in sports and piano. Beginning judo at age eleven, she received the final rank of brown belt (Ikkyu) before leaving for college overseas. During high school, Sarah joined the Hong Kong Police Marine as a girl scout and received formal training in police work such as criminal investigation in maritime smuggling.

Like her late father, Sarah inherited a deep sense of justice. This came to the forefront when, at the age of sixteen, Sarah became involved in a sexual assault case. A man publicly groped her friend's breast while on the street in one of Hong Kong's busiest districts. Sarah immediately sprang into action and pursued the fleeing suspect several blocks against oncoming traffic before flagging down a police officer, who arrested the man. Sarah testified before a British court, and the man was convicted. Although equipped with police training, she did not pursue criminal justice at university; instead, her natural talent for art won her heart.

After completing a bachelor's degree in art from Biola University (1993), Sarah, with only $40 in her pocket, began teaching herself to invest in the stock market, following in her mother's footsteps. Later, using the knowledge she learned from her mother and her own investigative research, Sarah invested the money from her employment to purchase several tech stocks (Yahoo and AOL) at their IPO prices. Selling most at their peak, just before the tech bubble burst, she invested her profits in mutual funds and real estate. Using the proceeds from her investments, Sarah purchased her first home at the age of 28. She accomplished this while also attending California State Polytechnic University, Pomona, obtaining her master's degree in business administration in 2002.

Although investing money was not something Sarah participated in until adulthood, she was ambitious and motivated enough to begin earning wages as a young person. At the tender age of twelve, Sarah began earning money through private tutoring. Using her earnings, she paid for her own piano lessons. After three years, she had saved enough money to purchase her first Yamaha piano. Music continued to be a passion that she pursued until her sophomore year in college. At a crossroads, she chose to devote her education to art, specializing in graphic design. A new field was emerging at that time: computer graphic design. As one of the first generation of graphic designers in this field, Sarah honed her skills in Adobe® products such as Photoshop® and Illustrator®. With her proficiency, Sarah was hired by her first full-time employer, Harte Hanks, and promoted several times within a year of graduating college.

By early 1994, a graphic production house recruited Sarah and she utilized her Photoshop® skills to complete high-profile publication projects for brands such as Gucci®, Prada, and Chanel®. By the fall of 1994, she began designing her own line of paper products such as greeting cards, journals, and notepads, which were sold by retailers such as Papyrus, Hallmark, and Jay Jacobs. In 2002, she started her first company with one of her former bosses as a partner, but in late 2004 the relationship soured. Sarah sold her share of the company to her partner and parted ways. As she left, she took nine boxes with her, samples of books she helped publish for self-publishers and independent authors. A fellow employee was so interested in continuing to work with Sarah, he left with her and offered to work for free at her new company. He became one of her first paid employees.

Parting ways with her former business partner opened new doors for Sarah. In October 2004, Sarah, with the help of her parents, established a new business: TSE Worldwide Press, Inc. Sarah's father patiently and strategically mentored her, and by 2007 she was running the U.S. operations herself, bringing in revenue exceeding $4 million. The other branch of the business, located in Hong Kong and operated by her siblings, controlled the manufacturing of the products and the logistics of international distribution. One night, in early 2008, Sarah had a dream in which she established a separate company, United Yearbook®, to expand her growing yearbook business. Not wasting any time, the following morning, Sarah registered United Yearbook® as a business with the Recorder's Office in San Bernardino, California. Although these professional business goals had become a reality, one personal goal still eluded her. Finally, after years of preparation, study, and perseverance, Sarah became a U.S. citizen in April 2009. To cap off her professional and personal achievements, in January 2018 United Yearbook® and its logo were officially registered with the U.S. Patent and Trademark Office and the Canadian Intellectual Property Office. Dreams do come true with prayers, perseverance, and hard work.

Once United Yearbook® was up and running, Sarah focused her attention on her law school studies from 2011 to 2014. These studies aided her immensely in her business acuity, as elucidated in the stories recounted in this book. By mid-2019, with the chaos and disorder in her business behind her, her companies became profitable again. Several lucrative contracts with new accounts have been secured, and the referrals and opportunities continue to roll in even as this book went to press.

Assisting her clients in expressing creativity and innovation, whether in their thinking and perspectives or in actualizing the products they desire to produce, creates immense fulfillment and joy for Sarah. An aggressive problem solver, Sarah refuses to quit. She takes pleasure in mentoring others in the art of self-publishing, especially first-time authors, as well as teenagers and community leaders such as police officers, school administrators and school teachers. Above all else, Sarah is passionate about sharing her faith in Christ and empowering people to see the God-given potential that resides in each and every one of us. Sarah's motto is "You can do it!"

ACKNOWLEDGMENTS

First, my special thanks to Dr. John K. Tuttle for believing in this project and helping me to create this book from my scattered thoughts into chronological order. It is amazing that we were able to complete the manuscript within three short months. I would not have been able to do it without your expertise, insights, and wise counsel.

I feel immense gratitude for my family, a circle of deeply united friends, university students, and colleagues from near and far who had a part in the creation of this book. I proudly list the following names of individuals who worked countless hours pouring out their souls and minds reading through the manuscript. I'm grateful for the time spent reviewing rounds of cover designs and imparting valuable input and advice: Marcela Archuleta, Alexis Au, Amy Chan, Jenny Chan Yee Yun, Belinda Chee, Clinton Chong, Daniel Chu, Seek Yee Chung, Josie DeCasas, Beth Allen Gehring, Loraine Kuk, Donna Ladner, Robin Kuehn Lawrence, Christina Lee, Pricilla Lee, Vincent Leung, Jimmy Lew, Sarah Li, Lily Limtiaco, Steve Limtiaco, Winnie Liu , Janet Lu, Ligia Mac, Professor Laureen Mgrdichian, Addie Mitz, Tiffany Ng, David S. Perez, Frances Pinzon, Takeo Shu, Diana Wang Sun, Olga Tian, Nancy Tse, David Wilson, Rubria A. Wilson, Chris Wong, Joanna Wu and Eric Yonemura.